THE
SWEETER
WELCOME

VOICES FOR A VISION OF AFFIRMATION:
BELLOW, MALAMUD AND MARTIN BUBER

THE SWEETER WELCOME

VOICES FOR A VISION OF AFFIRMATION:
BELLOW, MALAMUD AND MARTIN BUBER

ROBERT KEGAN

Humanitas
Press

The Sweeter Welcome
by Robert Kegan

Library of Congress catalog card number: 76-55860

ISBN: 0-911628-25-8

Printed in the United States of America

Humanitas Press
3 Wexford Street
Needham Heights
Massachusetts
02194

To my Mother and Father
for loving
each other

CONTENTS

ACKNOWLEDGMENTS

This got done. I take it as my reward that I can thank those people who are the reason it got done — even if I am hoping, as I do, that they know my feelings before and better than they see them here.

The book began at Dartmouth College during a year as a Senior Fellow. I am grateful to: the staff of Baker Library, my students in the Dartmouth Experimental College, and several members of Dartmouth's extraordinary English department. Professors Peter Bien and Blanche Gelfant were careful, critical readers of portions of the manuscript. So was Professor Arthur Jensen, who, in addition, was the Dean of the Senior Fellows, and in that capacity lent me congenially craggy support. No single person meant so much as Professor Alan Gaylord, whose belief sustained me and the project in a year when both were in peril. Because of him both got better. As fine teachers, all, these four folk were responsible *to* my work; they were not then, and are not now, responsible *for* it, or any of its many limitations.

Carolyn and I lived for several months in the Lubavitcher Hasidic Community of Crown Heights, Brooklyn. That we might come to feel connected to the turning of the earth, even the daily movement of darkness and light in this most urban of settings, we had no way of anticipating; that we might learn that "ritual" does not mean "empty ritual," or that community happens in time as well as space, we had no way of even understanding before we arrived. Education is a child of attention, but all attention is at least a mild form of surprise.

The Hasids may not care much for this book, at least not its "apparent reality." They were not fans of Buber's from the start. But, as before, this will matter to me more than it will to them, for they have had their own way of understanding my presence among them, and I have come to feel theirs is closer to the truth. Although we did not come for any deliberate purpose, least of all in connection with the present project, I was concerned that we be not falsely representing ourselves, and often mentioned I might eventually write something about my time with them. The reaction to this was always the same. Any explanation I gave for why I was there was politely accepted and clearly quite boring. "This is just what you say," was the essence of their response. "Your *nashomah,* your soul, has its own language, and its own way. That's what we are listening to." I hope they are still listening.

It was like that the whole time with the Lubavitchers, and it still is. Once when I returned to see some fellow students, the head of the Yeshivah, a rabbi who had always seemed somewhat stern, spied me in the corridor. "So it's Kegan," he said. I agreed that it was. "Back and forth, eh?" I stood before him somewhat sheepishly waiting for some comic barb about my spiritual vacillation. "It's just like the heart," he said, bringing his fist to his chest. "Back and forth, back and forth."

During many of the years this was being written I was receiving a kind of support from the Danforth Foundation that cannot be put in the bank. They waited around for me in a very important way, and will understand this peculiar thank-you.

As will Professor James Fowler, who takes seriously the fantasies of his friends.

Lester Mehling, Jill Orner, and Dorrie Freedman prepared the manuscript at various stages of its development. I was lucky to have such continually resourceful assistance.

There are others I want to mention whose support was important to me during the years I worked on this book: Saralee, Bernard, Larry, and Katherine; the Lyme community, Whipple district; Randy, Berent, and Astrid; many students, parents, teaching colleagues and their families at Saint Paul Academy and Summit School; and the Exeter-Melbourne Semi-Circle. One thing all of these had in common was their steady reminder that living itself makes mere diversion of these labors with language.

Throughout all these adventures one person, Carolyn, has joined me in them. (These days even gratitude itself might sound oppressive. "Sure she's given you so much that's special. Of course, But what have you really done for her?" Well, that's for her to say, in *her* book.) We were ourselves joined a few years ago by Lucia, whom we had one day, and who has been having us all the days since, I thank these two, my daughter and sun.

Finally, I thank those, not fools nor wise men, who neither rushed in nor feared to go; they are that larger, usually excluded middle, who just end up being there, probably at first because that's where the car was going while they were talking with someone in the back seat.

INTRODUCTION

In the third act of *Macbeth*, the King convenes a dinner party, and then, with proper pomp and plurals, excuses himself from the preliminaries:

> To make society the sweeter welcome
> We will keep ourselves till supper-time alone
> (III. i. 42-43).

The sweetness of community after the lean loneliness of its absence: that is what this book is about. We have withstood the winter long enough. We are near to enshrining this modern life, this modern literature of icy estrangement. This book spreads rumors of a thaw: of another kind of lettering, another philosophy — of modern folk to tell of a life of affirmation, human welcome, of community and embrace.

But why a *sweeter* welcome? This is a life not of mystical detachment, but of the noise and color of a smelly world; nor is it one of brave resignation, but of new discovery; and hence it is a richer life than the half-extended hand we have seen held out to us: for other people — even critics — have tried to tell of an end to our loneliness born of necessity, raised in defeat, and finally occupied with dissipation. The philosophy of Martin Buber in relation to the literary voices of Saul Bellow and Bernard Malamud offers us a sweeter welcome; not a welcoming *from* an old life, but a welcoming *to* a new one.

But really? Is it not true that Macbeth ends his loneliness by seeing things that are not there, and amazing his guests with his crazed carrying on? It will be, as always, for the reader to judge the appropriateness of these facts to the matter at hand.

Still, of what the book is not, a few things can be said by the author himself: This is not a study of Jewish novelists, nor even of Jewish novelists who use Jewish materials. It is not even, really, a study of Bellow or Malamud. It is rather a study of those of their books, in neither case their most recent, which, by striking purely what I hope to show is the essential chord of the Jewish genre, finally transcend their own materials to offer a new voice for contemporary fiction. It is a study of those books in light of Buber's thought. Why? One can say: in hopes that by bringing the works together the sweet welcome of each might be better conveyed. Or, risking the embarrassment, I (rather than "one") can say to you: to consort with the mysteries, found in relation, even between the written words of one man and the written words of another; finally, between the written word and our own unfolding.

But again about what the book is not: This is not a standard critical treatment of several novels. The question of a novel's form, for example, is not generally of central concern to this study. However, strange to the ear it may at this moment be, the focus is on the spirit of the novel. Spirit, Buber says, is "not in the I, but between I and Thou." The mystery of the universe, he suggests, may not be found so much in its many, special, and separate parts as in the spaces between, in the relationship of one part to another. The spirit of the novel is not in the novel, but between the novel and the reader. The concern, then, is with *relation*. A discussion of form, as an end in itself, generally leads only to the realm of *experience*. I have no interest in approaching the novel "to experience what there is to be experienced," as Buber says, in order to learn that "it is made in this way, or this is expressed in it, or its qualities are such and such, and further it takes this place in the scheme of things." If this approach to the novel needs defense, no less eminent a forebear than E. M. Forster can be enlisted as a spokesman. The novels under discussion here are possessed of what Forster chooses to call, in Aspects of the Novel, "fantasy," or "prophecy." Such novels, he says, "have gods," "a song," a certain "tone of voice," and it is important that they "be saved from the claws of critical apparatus." Such novels are "more than time or people or logic or any of their derivatives, more even than Fate. And by 'more' I do not mean something that excludes these aspects nor something that includes them, embraces them. I mean something that cuts across them like a bar of light, that is intimately connected with them at one place . . . and at another place shoots over or through them as if they did not exist."

It is this "bar of light" we are about. How else should we avoid doing damage of death to the very mystery we wish to preserve and celebrate? What could be worse than to "understand" these books, to speed them along to the junkheap of Furies absorbed by a Liberal Nation: "Every fury on earth," James Agee wrote, "has been absorbed in time, as art, or as religion, or as authority in one form or another. The deadliest blow the enemy of the human soul can strike is to do fury honor." Melting pots have been occasions of loss from the very beginning: "And Moses turned, and went down from the mount. . . . And when Joshua heard the noise of the people as they shouted, he said unto Moses '. . . *It is not the voice of them that shout for mastery, neither is it the voice of them that cry for being overcome . . .'*" (Exodus xxxii. 15-18). And where today is the voice of mastery, of mystery, of being overcome? The pitch, the timbre, the rhythm of the voice — does it come now only from the men on the mountain, the mouth of the poet, the corners of life? And where are our teachers, our *zaddikim,* our Hasidim, our chariots of God? Well, they are not in the "synagogue": the man behind the pulpit is more likely to be a scratch-handicap complimentary member of the country club.

We have withstood the winter long enough. This book spreads rumors of a thaw, of a hopemaking amidst the brokenness of the world. The mystery lives and waits to reproduce itself, and in this hope there may yet be a reason to write about art, to tell stories to stories. Can art give back to life that which it has rescued from it? So emerges a purpose for criticism: to keep the art from being "understood." "That before which, in which, out of which, and into which we live, even the mystery, has remained what it was. It has become present to us as salvation; we have 'known' it, but we acquire no knowledge from it which might lessen or moderate its mysteriousness. We have come near to God, but no nearer to unveiling being or solving its riddle. We have felt release, but not discovered a 'solution.' We can only go and confirm its truth . . ." we can, we *must.*

SH'MA YISRAEL
THE VOX CLAMANTIS

The Jews — they drop on anything at any moment, and that sort of thing makes the mystic in the end.[1]
— Djuna Barnes

Liberty in America has meant so far the breaking away from *all* dominion. The true liberty will only begin when Americans discover IT, and proceed directly to fulfill IT. IT being the deepest *whole* self of man, the self in its wholeness, the whole soul.[2]

— D. H. Lawrence

"I'm trying to figure out who this Thou is."
— Wilhelm, in Saul Bellow's *Seize the Day* [3]

All great religious traditions have developed mystical movements. There has never been a case in which this development did not involve a revolt against the doctrines or practices of orthodoxy — with one exception. Hasidism, a mystical movement of Judaism, became as committed as Jewish orthodoxy itself to the all-pervasive rigor of Jewish law; to the thoroughly intellective enterprise of Talmudic study.[4] While at first punished, and later scorned by orthodoxy, Hasidism itself finds no obstacle in orthodoxy to its intense and ecstatic apprehension of the holy; more than this, it has considered orthodoxy's discipline and rationality a necessity, in need rather of fertilization and mystical appropriation than reform or abandonment. Today it is not uncommon, as I have seen in my own experiences living with the Hasidim, for an *orthodox* Jew traveling in a strange town — an individual who may have no feeling and less sympathy for mystical Judaism — to "stay by" *Hasidic* families in order to assure himself of a proper meal in accordance with the strictures of dietary law. And today, Jewish and non-Jewish media alike refer to the *mystical* sect, apparently with no sense of the irony of the expression or the uniqueness of the phenomenon, as the "ultra-orthodox."

When a mystical movement comes to represent the ultimacy of orthodoxy, when the passionate and the rational are cohabiting so nicely, unusual offspring must be the result. The Jewish genre of contemporary fiction has provided us with works drawn from a medley of Jewish circumstance. But some few of these works have struck general readers and critics alike as possessing special powers; as being, at the same time, more in touch with, and transcendent of, their Jewish materials; as saying something of unusual importance to us and to the course of contemporary fiction. My interest is to suggest how these special novels grow out of this uncommon marriage, are reflective of a vision at once intensely particular, the flower of an ancient tradition, and at the same time directly responsive — even offering of resolution — to the diverse exercises of the modern soul we now call existentialism. Companions to a qualitative reconstruction of our contemporary situation, the novels come to feel like the beginning of a new voice in the American novel of this century.

To place these works more clearly in this broader context, let me say a little about the literary and philosophic personality of the last seventy-five years. It is generally accepted that the twentieth-century novel made a distinctive break with its past. We even agree on the cause, and say, with our usual self-regard, that our century, compared to others, lacks a certain stability. Though not insensitive to the anguish of enduring in the days of Fielding or Defoe, we do point out that they at least had some order to their anguish: a background of fact and value given and taken by reader and writer alike.

The significance this has for the artist — in terms of where he or she begins and the kinds of questions he or she asks — is total: "In a stable culture" — this from Dorothy Van Ghent — "the artist inherits certain broad assumptions as to the nature of reality, and the kind of relationships people maintain with themselves, with each other, and with their natural environment. The subjective, introspective impulse is then quiescent; there is no spiritual need on the part of the individual to go questing backward over his personal life in an attempt to find in it a meaningful form or unity or direction; for his social environment objectively manifests to him a form, a unity, a direction that correspond with his feelings."[5]

In the twentieth century, form, unity, direction — the structure within which the individual and the novel spent their cycle — ceased to exist. "Things," as Yeats says, "fall apart; the center cannot hold,/Mere anarchy is loosed upon the world." Having thus announced the falling apart of things, the twentieth century, like all the king's horses and all the king's men, turned to the questions of if and how things might be put back together again. From this examination there developed answers, refusals to answer, and much mere contemplation of the questions. Taken together these comprise our century's personal philosophy, existentialism.[6]

Of the things that fell apart, the most important was our connection to a supersensible reality. The vertical thrust to life came crashing down, and the thud, deprived of the third dimension, spread itself over the skin of the earth. "We are down where all ladders start," Yeats again, "in the foul rag-and-bone shop of the heart." Confronted with a horizontal world, this flatland, this North Dakota uninformed by superhuman direction, twentieth-century folk ask the existential question: "Given that there is nothing 'up there,' what is down here?"

Risking the overly simple in hopes of the heuristic, I am going to suggest that, for some time, the various answers to this question took shape in two richly heterogeneous but clearly distinguishable forms; and further, that for some time the underlying vision to be found in the literature of our century was similarly divisible. I am going to take a little time to explore these visions — of "alienation" and "accommodation" — mostly by attending in each case to a novel that brings that vision to life. These prepare the way for a new arrival, a qualitative transformation, a third spiritual organization of our mutually agreed-upon condition. Like the others, it has developed its own existential school, inspired by a particular existential philosopher; and, like the others, its vision has begun to find a symbolic life in the pulse of the particular, the contemporary novel. Unlike the others, its source reaches back into that history which is itself a parent of existentialism; and so, gathering this modern discussion at its roots, is able perhaps to find a voice of greater resonance. It is a voice of affirmation. It rises out of the existential school of neo-Hasidism; its spokesman is Martin Buber; its literary companions occupy our attentions in the chapters to come.

"Given that there is nothing 'up there,' what is down here?" — the position we are calling alienation, whose overwhelming influence on the intellectual and aesthetic life of this century has become so clear to us that it is hard not to look at the word itself as a cliché, answers the question by saying, "Nothing. Meaninglessness. Man is a stranger to his universe, to his fellowman, and to himself. Existence is utterly absurd." Jean Paul Sartre, perhaps unwillingly, became the leading spokesman for this position. "Man is the being," he said, "by whom Nothingness comes into being."[7] In Sartre's "being-in-itself" and "being-for-itself" dichotomy there is no ground of being in which two people can come together, know one another, give to one another, love one another. The literary representations of this position are abundant. Eric and Mary Josephson write in *Man Alone*: "The consciousness of estrangement and loneliness . . . the alienated hero — this mood colors the poetry of Yeats, Rilke, Pound, Eliot; it figures in the works of Gide, Kafka, Thomas Mann, Hemingway, Thomas Wolfe, Alberto Moravia, and Sartre — to the alienated man as seen by these authors, life is essentially meaningless or absurd."[8]

One thinks further of Joseph Conrad's *Secret Agent*, one of the finest and least discussed irrational novels of the century; of Sinclair Lewis, whose Babbitt world is as accusingly meaningless and unsaved as it was when he saw it forty-five years ago; of Virginia Woolf, who presents in the Mrs. Dalloway/Septimus figure as full a picture of an empty being, as vital a story of spiritual death, as any of her peers; of William Golding's child islands and lofty spires loudly crashing into nothing; of Evelyn Waugh, who, beginning with just a handful of dust, shapes a wasteland all his own; of the dramatists — Brecht and Beckett, Ionesco, and Genet.

What happens to a person's energy — to his or her spirit — in an alienated world? There is perhaps no finer vision of the condition than the one we see through William Faulkner, in his achingly beautiful novel *The Sound and the Fury.*[9] In telling this story of the Compson family's decay, Faulkner forces us to confront continually the movement of energy around a circle. The book is so structured that two circles — what I will call "the circle of time" and "the circle of passion" — are fit, one upon the other, with a brilliant result. The circle of passion describes a situation where one's feelings come back to their source, where they fail to connect to the person or thing that is loved, where they do not release sparks, but run back on themselves. The circle of time refers to a situation where tomorrow and tomorrow creeps into yesterday, where every so often it is the same moment, the same time it was a while ago. The face of a clock is, of course, the best symbol of such a phenomenon, where, as Quentin Compson says, "every hour it's a quarter to something again" (p. 212).

Fit, one upon the other, the two circles together illustrate perfectly the true terror of alienation: the imprisonment of spiritual circularity. At some moment in time my feelings are sent out to a loved one; time passes, and then one day that event, carrying those feelings, comes crashing back into me; there I stand, my feelings never having gotten where I wanted them to go; there I stand, back at the time when I originally sent them out. With a sound and a fury fertilizing nothing the feelings go pumping around the circle. "All you had done," as Quentin says, "were shadows all you had felt suffered took visible form antic and perverse mocking without relevance inherent themselves with the denial of the significance they should have affirmed" (p. 211).

Benjy Compson, as an idiot, is the human personification of this circle. His memories are as real and immediate to him as the events of the present. His reveries are perfect examples of feeling running into itself. When Benjy sees Miss Quentin and the man from the carnival sitting together on the swing, he relives an event twenty years earlier when he ached with love for his sister Caddy, sitting on the swing with Charlie. No matter how far apart the two events actually are, they are concurrent for Benjy, simultaneously enduring the anguish of his intense experiences. Who receives the feelings of Benjy, sent out at one point in time? No one but Benjy, at another point in time.

The same is true of Quentin Compson. He simultaneously

experiences a fight with Gerald Bland on a picnic and a fight with Dalton Ames sometime earlier. In both cases he is sending feeling to his sister. But the passions of the one event communicate only with the passions of the other. They are trapped in the circle. Only Quentin Compson receives the feelings of Quentin Compson. By framing this episode in violence — the fistfights — Faulkner tips us off as to the necessary end to life lived on a circle.

The artist presents one of the most lovely and concise demonstrations of the circle in a pathetic scene with Benjy, standing near a fence, sending out feelings to his sister: "Caddy, Caddy, Caddy," he shouts through the fence. But on the other side of the fence, men are playing golf, and they send his feelings back to him in a perverse echo, shouting, "Caddie, caddie, caddie" (p.1). "All I had felt suffered taking form antic and perverse mocking without relevance."

This same kind of unusual return of the object of passion happens to Quentin, now a college man, when his sister — in all her innocence — returns to him, in the form of an Italian waif. "Hello, sister," he says to her when she approaches (p. 155). He then commences to take the girl with whom he cannot speak around the town with which he is not familiar. There is not a moment of communication. Not a single message gets through. All possibility of passionate connection is outrageously parodied in the character of the little girl's preposterous brother. There will be no incest. There has been no love.

What, then, is the result of life on the circle — of a person's spirit never creating, never doing work, never reaching another, flowing only back onto itself? Violence, decay, death. And why? Quentin, at the end of his day, dresses for a rendezvous with the only being he could ever love — not Caddy, as so many think, but himself. Life on the circle becomes finally an attempt at self-fertilization and there is only one way to make it with yourself: for Quentin Compson suicide becomes the consummate act of self-love.

The novel of alienation is the literary correlate for one general answer to the existential question "Given there is nothing 'up there,' what is down here?" The position of accommodation represents a second general answer. The accommodationist replies, "Not much, but the human community is possible. Existence probably is absurd absolutely, but it is not meaningless nor is it unsatisfying."[10] I can find meaning and pleasure in life, the accommodationist says — moreover, I can keep my spirit from destroying me — if I will channel that spirit into an artificial system. Answers of this sort organize around the philosophical inspiration of Albert Camus. His reinterpretation of the myth of Sisyphus concisely defines the accommodationist position. In the original tale, Sisyphus was condemned by the gods to push a huge boulder to the top of a hill, only to have it roll down the other side. Sisyphus spent his entire life at this fruitless task. The reinterpretation by Camus finds Sisyphus a happy man: "Sisyphus concludes that all is well. The universe — though without a master — seems neither sterile nor futile. Each atom of that stone, each mineral flake of that night-filled mountain, in itself forms a world. The struggle itself is enough to fill a man's heart."[11]

Here given its most positive reading, the position of accommodation claims that we can live out useful lives — can anyway keep from killing ourselves — if we will adhere to a system, take pleasure in the work itself, and not spend time considering an end or purpose for it.

In his book *After Alienation*, Marcus Klein argues that this position represents a true end to the chronicle by and of modern folk adrift. As authors representative of the position, in one way or another, he lists William Styron, Vance Bourjaily, Harvey Swados, R. V. Cassill, George P. Elliot, Flannery O'Connor, John Cheever, John Updike, and Herbert Gold.[12] In the body of his work, Klein discusses the fiction of Wright Morris, Ralph Ellison, and James Baldwin — all of whom I would agree are accommodationist.[13] (Klein also includes, quite unfortunately, the fiction of Saul Bellow and Bernard Malamud — much of whose work, it is argued in pages to come, is anything but accommodationist.) In addition to these men, one thinks of such varied fiction as John Steinbeck's *Winter of Our Discontent*, Richard Farina's *Been Down So Long It Looks Like Up to Me*, and *A Long and Happy Life*, by Reynolds Price, all of which reflect an accommodationist vision.

But this position, taken for what it really is — a giving up, a giving in; an end to marching through the desert not because we are out of the desert, but because there is nothing *but* desert — this position is not in any way so conclusive or satisfactory, even in its own terms, as Camus, Klein, and others would insist. As the best proof of this, and to explore the accommodationist vision brought to life, I select a novel that was intended as an endorsement of the position — *The Guard of Honor* by James Gould Cozzens. [14] Cozzens's wonderfully readable World War II tale of three days on a Florida air force base uses the military as a vibrant symbol of an artificial system that a man must accommodate. Energy is channeled: to what end, exactly, is not clear. Colonel Mowbray asks for clarifying memos, but, not getting them, is not impeded from doing his work (p. 49). A young designer says, "When they don't tell you what they want it for you can't be sure"; still this doesn't bother his progress (p. 132). The idea is not so much that energy be expended toward a purpose as that energy merely be expended in a "useful way," that men be, as Colonel Ross says, "usefully employed" (p. 60).

Cozzens's description of one of his main perceivers, Captain Hicks, shows Hicks to be a modern Sisyphus: "He belonged to that undistinguished majority of men," Cozzens writes, "for whom it should no doubt be a mortification that work was an end in itself, not a necessary detested means to make a living, certainly not a shrewd enterprise whose motive and hope was some blissful state of living without work. His bliss was here and now; there was no pastime like the press of business" (p. 120).

But for all his attempts to endorse the system — to make heroes of those persons who understand its machinations, the compromises that must be made, the evils that must be accommodated — Cozzens, in the end, unwittingly shows the system to be a dissipator, a dehumanizer, an institution that makes us finally less than persons.

General Beal and Benny Carricker, for example, whom Cozzens demeaningly postures as children, really emerge not *as* children, but *like* children, in the sense that they have something children have — a spirit. As an exceptional officer, Beal has had to accommodate very little. He spends much of his time trying to accommodate even less, trying to emulate Benny, who is so extraordinary he has not had to accommodate anything or anyone. For all his brashness and impulsiveness, Benny displays more sympathy, more loyalty, more human feeling than any other character in the book. Beal, in trying desperately to keep his spirit from being dissipated in the system, revolts by taking his airplane up for a spin in the middle of a crisis. But in trying to take it "as high as she'll go" he is unable to take her high enough; the heavy pull of the system brings him down to earth, forces him to accommodate, leaving us with a sense of loss.

Cozzens's heroes, on the other hand, are in the end half-men, effete, spiritless. Colonel Ross, the aging judge, is not up in the sky when problems call. He is a realist, a smoother-over, a man with the serenity to accept those things he cannot change. But in the book's last scene, when the weekend's crisis is over and averted, General Beal thinks to himself that only two men were foolish enough to get upset. One is an acknowledged dolt. The other is Colonel Ross, and "well," Beal thinks, "who was he?" This must be our last impression of Ross, as well. How much of a man is he really? He never once in the book follows his own conscience at the expense of the system. His feeling about the discrimination against "Negro personnel" is that it certainly is unjust, that things should and may change one day. Yet he himself admits it is the system that preserves the injustice, and he spends his every moment preserving the system.

Cozzens's other hero, Captain Hicks, is equally pathetic. Painted by the author as a man to be admired — a man, like Sisyphus, who will obediently do research on a flight manual knowing full well that upon completion it will be thrown out — Hicks is as devoid of spirit as Colonel Ross. His one indiscretion, his one puny display of feeling, is that — a married man — he quickly, sadly, almost therapeutically has sex with WAC Lieutenant Amanda Turck. The system is, of course, willing to accommodate *him* for this naughtiness, if he will continue to jump when called, if he will respond to a phone call eight minutes after coitus, rush onto an airplane, and continue work for the system. This he does.

Who is Hicks? He is the accommodationist version of the maker. Not a writer — "Don't mix me up with writers," he says — he is an editor. He creates nothing. He fits things to the page.

But more telling even than the reversal of his characters is Cozzens's choice for an accommodationist model. Offered as a way out of the night, a nondestructive release for man's spirit, an answer to human violence, accommodation, truly portrayed in *Guard of Honor* fulfills not one of these needs.

Purportedly putting an end to the human dissolution and denigration — the waste — of our alienation, the accommodationist offers us a smooth operation, a well-run system, a process to keep minds usefully employed. Yet more horrible than the fact that it all goes on at the cost of human talents, more ironic than the fact that to avoid the waste of private despair persons choose the waste of public process — more horrible and ironic than this is that all through *Guard of Honor,* behind the hum of this well-tooled machine, is the unconfronted truth: it all exists for the very purpose of *doing* violence, of turning people into dirt, of making war.

Alienation and accommodation — spiritual circularity and spiritual dissipation — these comprise the answers thus far received to the question "Given nothing 'up there,' what is down here?"

There is another answer. There is affirmation: "Everything! It's all down here. We may be living without the vertical. We may live on the horizontal. But the horizontal is holy." "The key is in the sunlight," Ginsberg's "Kaddish" tells us, and the spirit in which he offers his poem is the same spirit in which the universal mystery of the Hasid is offered to those who agonize in the desert:

> Take this, this psalm from me
> Burst from my hand in a day . . .
> This is the End
> The Redemption from Wilderness
> Way for the Wanderer
> House sought for all . . . [15]

Take this, this psalm from me: "Over against all this behavior of present day man Hasidism sets the simple truth that the wretchedness of our world is grounded in its resistance to the entrance of the holy into lived life."[16]

Martin Buber, the man who speaks the words above, developed for the twentieth century the blend of passion and rationality that characterized the mysticism of the eighteenth-century sect. The result, neo-Hasidism, emerges from the center of existential tradition yet dramatically moves moderns from the mire of our indecision.

To the answers of concession, to those who speak of alienation and accommodation, to Sartre and Camus, Buber responds with strength and clarity: "Those who contemplate the cruel problematic as a subject of unsurpassable interest, who know how to describe and even perhaps to praise it, contribute at times with the highest gifts, to the massive decisionlessness whose true name is the decision for nothing." [17]

Neo-Hasidism, historically and temperamentally, represents the flowering of existentialism — whose seeds were originally sown when Hebrew met Hellene. "The impact of Hebrew faith on the Hellenistic world," writes Harvey Cox, "was to 'temporalize' the dominant perception of reality. The world *became* history. *Cosmos* became *aeon*; *mundus* ('world' in a space sense) became *saeculum* ('world' in a time sense)." [18] I should be quick to point out that in emphasizing a distinction between the Greek and Hebraic, Cox, William Barrett, and others, have perhaps distorted the ideals of both. And though one may want to substitute "Platonism" or "Aristotelianism" for what Barrett calls "Hellenism," there is, I think, some value — particularly from the standpoint of Hasidism — to the dichotomy he sets up:

(1) The ideal man of Hebraism is the man of faith; for Hellenism . . . the man of reason.

(2) The man of faith is the concrete man in his wholeness; Hebraism does not raise its eyes to the universal and abstract; its vision is always of the concrete, particular, individual man. The Greeks, on the other hand, were the first thinkers in history, they discovered the universal, the abstract and timeless essences, forms, and ideas.

(3) There is for the Greek the ideal of *detachment* . . . the Hebraic emphasis is on *commitment*, the passionate involvement of man with his own mortal being (at once flesh and spirit), with his offspring, family, tribe, and God

(4) For the Greek . . . man is the animal of connected logical discourse. For the Hebrew . . . intellect and logic are the pride of fools and do not touch the ultimate issues of life, which transpire at a depth that language can never reach, the ultimate depth of fate. [19]

"The features of Hebraic man," Barrett writes, "are those which existential philosophy has attempted to exhume and bring to the reflective consciousness of our time."[20] And existentialism has done this, but it has done this inconclusively. The answers of alienation and accommodation emphasize, to an extent, the Hebraic directions. But the answer of Hasidism, the affirmative answer, itself a child of Hebraism, is quite naturally better able to bring "the features of Hebraic man . . . to the reflective consciousness of our time." Without wanting to romanticize the Jewish experience, it does not seem outlandish to suggest that in Barrett's summary of the "existential problematic" we hear something of Jewish history as well: "man's feeling of homelessness, of alienation, of estrangement; a sense of the basic fragility and contingency of human life; the impotence of reason confronted with the depth of existence; the threat of Nothingness; and the solitary and unsheltered condition of the individual before his threat."[21] But, inevitably, to say that thirty-five centuries of Jewishness now find reflection in the preoccupations of modern persons — Jew and non-Jew — for the shape of reality, a way home, "identity" — to say this is to dwell in the desert, if not in the dust of cliché. Jewishness, existentialism — we, ourselves — are more than this, and deserve a better representative. More than Egyptian bondage, more than forty years of desert, existentialism, driven to its deepest dimension, yields a third answer. And if some contribution special to the modern condition is to be sought from the Jew, perhaps one should turn not to a voice that decides for the dark with more poignance than those around it but to one that signals a way out of the night.

Born in Eastern Europe in the eighteenth century, Hasidism is the mystical faith begun by "unenlightened" Polish and Ukrainian Jewry who, according to Buber, "brought forth the greatest phenomenon in the history of the spirit, greater than any individual genius in art and in thought: a society that lives by its faith."[22]

The fundamental principle of Hasidism is that "God can be beheld in each thing and in each pure deed."[23] From this, all else proceeds: the hallowing of the everyday:

All that man possesses conceals sparks which belong to the root of his soul and wish to be elevated by him to their origin . . . in the era before creation these sparks had fallen into all things and are now imprisoned in them until ever again a man uses a thing in holiness and thus liberates the sparks that it conceals.[24]

What is the essential point of Hasidism — that man exerts influence on the external, and that this is not done by any special works, but by the intention with which he does all his works. It is the teaching of the hallowing of the everyday. The issue is not to attain a new type of acting which, owing to its object, would be sacred or mystical; the issue is to do the one appointed task, the common obvious tasks of daily life according to their truth and according to their meaning.[25]

the dissolution of division between the sacred and the profane:

The profane is regarded only as a preliminary stage of the holy; it is the not-yet-hallowed . . . . At each place, each hour, in each act, in each speech the holy can blossom forth.[26]

the mutual neediness of person and concrete world:

It is only when it is brought into actual contact with the individual that the world becomes sacramental. That is, in the actual contact of these things and beings with this individual, with you, with me. In all of these things and beings dwells the divine spark, and all of these things and beings are given to this particular individual that this particular individual may through his contact with them redeem the divine spark. Man's existence in the world becomes fraught with meaning because the things and beings of the world have been given to him in their sacramental potentiality . . . The Hasidic world is the concrete world as it is in this moment of a person's life; it is a world ready to be a sacrament.[27]

"horizontal" identification with the divine, the rejection of the sublimation of man in God:

> Hallowing is an event which commences in the depths of man, there where choosing, deciding, beginning takes place. The man who thus begins enters into the hallowing. But he can only do this if he begins as man and presumes to no superhuman holiness. The true hallowing of a man is the hallowing of the human in him.[28]

> Meeting with God does not come to man in order that he may concern himself with God, but in order that he may confirm that there is *meaning in the world*.[29]

"Man cannot approach the divine," Buber writes, "by reaching beyond the human; he can approach Him through becoming human. To become human is what he, this individual man, has been created for. This, so it seems to me," says Buber, "is the eternal core of Hasidic life and of Hasidic learning."[30]

And Hasidic life and Hasidic learning are the eternal core of Judaism: "By its fundamental principle of the actual acceptance of God in things," Buber says, "the Hasidic message completes and widens the ancient teaching of Israel. It is a completion. In all sections of the Law do we find 'Be ye holy, even as I am holy,' not as a command for the gradual sanctification of mankind apart from things, but as a command that mankind as its contribution towards creation shall step by step sanctify things." But it is also a widening: "In ancient Israel the sacrifice was the cultural sister of the meal, which could not exist without it; the sacrifice was a sanctification of a part of the very same organic matter of which the rest was given to men for their nourishment. In the Hasidic life it is the eating itself which becomes a sacramental service."[31] "Nowhere," Buber says, in *Jewish Mysticism*, "has the spiritual power of Judaism made itself felt in the last centuries as among the Hasids. The old power lives in it which once bound down the Eternal to eartn, so that it might be realized in daily life; and thus, without changing an iota of the old Law, the ritual, or the tradition of daily life, what had become old can live again in a new light and expression."[32] What came to live again was "a mysticism which became the possession of the people."[33]

This mysticism is composed of four separate but interdependent stances and these stances, dynamic, tending toward each other, comprise an essence of Hasidism, and the soul of the novels we will examine. Given their Hebrew names, they are *hitlahabut*, or ecstacy; *aboda*, work, service, or devotion; *kavana*, intention; and *shiflut*, humility. *Hitlahabut* is "the burning, the ardour of ecstasy. A fiery sword guards the tree of Life. It is extinguished by *hitlahabut*, whose lightest touch vanquishes it. The road is open."[34] The Open Road: the rogue's home: Saul Bellow proves the picaresque to be the perfect vessel for *hitlahabut* — and *hitlahabut* to be the perfect vessel for the picaresque.[35] "The world is no more ecstasy's habitation," Buber writes, "ecstasy is the habitation of the world."[36]

Aboda is "the service of God in time and space."[37] *Aboda* asks, "What am I and what is my life?"[38] "If a man collects himself," Buber says, "and becomes at one with himself, then he draws near to the unity of God. . . . This is *aboda*."[39] *The Assistant* and *The Fixer* are novels of *aboda*, of fragmented men collecting themselves and becoming at one. They are ultimately novels about serving time.[40]

Kavana is the "mystery of a soul consecrated on a single aim."[41] It will be enough to say here that *kavana* is Frank Alpine "trying to figure out why they were the Chosen People,"[42] "doing it with discipline and with love";[43] is Yakov Bok, "trying to comprehend what was happening and explain it to himself."[44] *Kavana* is Augie March "hoping to be still so that the axial lines can be found";[45] is Henderson's "disturbance in the heart, a voice that spoke there and said, *I want, I want, I want!*"[46] *Kavana* is that need which compels Herzog, which compels Bellow himself: "the need to explain, to have it out, to justify, to put in perspective, to make amends."[47]

Shiflut is the mystery of a certain kind of humility, "no willed and practiced virtue. It is nothing but an inner being, feeling, and expressing. Nowhere in it is there a compulsion, nowhere a self-humbling, a self-restraining, a self-resolve. It is indivisible as the glance of a child and simple and a child's speed."[48] We must leave it to later chapters to explore whether the books, inside themselves and in the spaces they share with the reader, have to do with "the feeling of the community of existence. To feel the universal generation as a sea, and oneself as a wave in it, this is the mystery of humility."[49]

Hitlahabut, aboda, kavana, shiflut — these organize the life of the Hasidim. What that life is like we might begin to understand through the Hasidic folktale or legend. Of these tales Buber says, "At the base of them lies the stammering of inspired witnesses who witnessed to what befell them, to what they comprehended, as well as to what was incomprehensible to them." [50]

To complete this introduction to the foundation of the mystery we have been seeking all along, to show the origins of Buber's philosophy of *I and Thou*, to offer literature for comparison to the affirmative novel's antecedents (which I will later introduce), and to offer literature for comparison to the affirmative novel itself, I present a few of these tales in full:

> Once Zalman interrupted his prayers and said: "I do not want your paradise. I do not want your coming world. I want You, and You only." [51]

A disciple of Rabbi Shmelke's begged his master to teach him how to prepare his soul for the service to God. The *zaddik* told him to go to Rabbi Hayyim, who — at that time — was still an innkeeper. The disciple did as he was bidden and lived in the inn for several weeks without observing any vestige of holiness in the innkeeper, who from the morning prayer till night devoted himself to his business. Finally he asked him what he did all day. "My most important occupation," said Rabbi Hayyim, "is to clean the dishes properly, so that not the slightest trace of food is left, and to clean and dry the pots and pans, so that they do not rust." When the disciple returned home and reported to Rabbi Shmelke what he had seen and heard, the rabbi said to him: "Now you know the answer to what you asked me." [52]

The psalm reads: "For singing to our God is good." Rabbi Elimelekh expounded thus: "It is good if man can bring about that God sings within him." [53]

Whatever the rabbi of Koznitz said sounded as if he were praying, only weaker and in a lower voice. He liked to hum to himself proverbs and sayings current among the Polish peasants. After a Purim feast, which he had presided over in great happiness, he said: "How right, what the people say: 'doff your coat, dear soul, and prance/Merrily at feast and dance.' But how curious a coat is the body!"

Sometimes he even spoke to God in Polish. When he was alone, they would hear him say: "*Moj kochanku*," which means: "My darling." [54]

The rabbi of Berditchev used to sing a song, of which is as follows:

>Where I wander — You!
>Where I ponder — You!
>Only You, You again, always You!
>You! You! You!
>When I am gladdened — You!
>When I am saddened — You!
>Only You, You again, always You!
>You! You! You!
>Sky is You! Earth is You!
>You above! You below!
>In every trend, at every end,
>Only You, You again, always You!
>You! You! You! [55]

Seized by this spirit of Hasidism — by this intense and immediate apprehension of the divine, of the holy in all things and all acts — Buber was driven to his epiphany: "I saw human life," he says, "as the possibility of a dialogue with being."[56] Gathering this truth and those from which it derives, blended with the needs and reason of the twentieth century, Buber conceived what has since come to be known as neo-Hasidism. "I saw human life as the possibility of a dialogue with being": this idea, springing from the first expressions of Hebrew thought as evidenced in the story of Job, protected in the mystical writings of the Cabala, nurtured by the faith and fervor of an obscure eighteenth-century sect, and finally seeing the light of modern day in the work of Martin Buber — this idea, religiously and philosophically ancient and modern — gives words to the mystery that is the essence of Jewishness. (It is not for nothing that novels reflective of the vision seem somehow more in touch with their Jewish materials.)

Yet neo-Hasidism has its beginnings in Hebraism,[57] where all existential thought has its beginnings; and, as such, its presuppositions are the same as those of other existential systems: the ladder *is* gone, we really *must* "lie down where all ladders start/In the foul rag-and-bone shop of the heart," the individual *is* a stranger, he or she *does* "stand face to face with a flat and inexplicable world." (It is not for nothing that "Jewish" novels reflective of the neo-Hasidic affirmation seem somehow to have transcended their parochial materials.) But with these presuppositions, twentieth-century thought and literature, having left the false gods of the Egyptians behind, took steps into the desert and floundered there.

Neo-Hasidism points a way out. The human heart, Buber seems to be saying to Yeats, and to Sartre as well, is the place from which we should have started all along; and in the foul rag-and-bone shop a new vision is being pieced together with the same materials. Quoting from Sartre's *Situations,* that God "is dead [in that] He spoke to us and now is silent; all that we touch now is His corpse," Buber thinks that if we "realize what it means to live in an age of such a concealment, such a divine silence, we shall perhaps understand its implications for our existence as something entirely different from that which Sartre desires to teach us."[58] What he desires to teach us, Buber goes on, is clear. It is, in Sartre's words, that "this silence of the transcendent, combined with the perseverance of the religious need in modern man, is the great concern today as yesterday. It is the problem which torments Nietzsche, Heidegger, Jaspers."[59] But "the problem that 'torments' the existentialist thinker of our age," Buber replies, "lies deeper than Sartre thinks."

It focuses finally in the question of whether the perseverance of the "religious need" does not indicate something inherent in human existence. Does existence really mean, as Sartre thinks, existing "for oneself" encapsuled in one's own subjectivity? Or does it not essentially mean standing *over against* the X — not an X for which a certain quality could be substituted, but rather the X itself, the undefinable and unfathomable? "God," says Sartre, "is the quintessence of the Other." But the Other for Sartre is he who "looks at" me, who makes me into an object, as I make him. . . . But what if God is not the quintessence of the Other, but rather its absoluteness?

And what if it is not primarily the reciprocal relation of subject and object which exists between me and the other, but rather the reciprocal relation of I and Thou? [60]

Wandering a desert, with no imaginative place from which to see that wandering other than the Egypt I have left behind, makes of me a deserter. Buber stands in the same desert as we; it could not be otherwise. But sighting, as he does, the "way for the wanderer, House sought for all," he ends exiling to take up other kinds of work, difficult, but yet free of Sartre's sterile isolation. He is heading for home. We might say heading to a *promised land*, but then we must try to catch Buber's own spirit in a word like *promise*. There is *that which we are promised*, but there is also about the word our own answer, *our promise, that which we might become*. The land Buber sights is full of this kind of conversation, one he wishes Sartre might hear, Sartre who "has started from the silence of God without asking himself what part our not hearing and our not having heard has played in that silence."[61]

If Buber's neo-Hasidic vision is brought to blood and bones in the novels we are about to explore, there is little point to our spending much time on the philosophy here, when there are people and places waiting to be met on the pages that follow. Still, in order to avoid the sort of misunderstanding not at all uncommon (especially among those who have made Buber a folk hero, which in America is to say that his words, ironically, have become products), it will be helpful to examine for just a moment the nature of those needs to which Hasidism — through Buber — has responded.

A modern dilemma seems to be that we desperately need, on the one hand, to be reunited with the sacred (to have faith in faith), while, on the other hand, we need to have our faith in reason go unmolested. The genius of Hasidism, translated for all people in Buber's neo-Hasidism, is that its form safeguards reason, releasing us to the content — and the sacred. We have said already that when God died He took meaning along with Him, leaving modern folk lost in the desert. And we have said too that the neo-Hasidic "Jew," long a wanderer in the desert, points the way to Canaan by pointing in the place *between* — where God, outsmarting (and outliving) Nietzsche, was really hiding all along. While the words of neo-Hasidism may point the way to the sacred, it is the shape of neo-Hasidism, giving a place to reason, that moves man in the direction Buber points.

To understand better the way in which neo-Hasidism does respond to both of these needs let us look briefly at a few passages from *I and Thou* :

> It is said that man experiences his world. What does that mean?
> Man travels over the surface of things and experiences them. He extracts knowledge about their construction from them: he wins an experience from them. He experiences what belongs to the things. [62]

> This and the like together establish the realm of *It*.
> But the realm of *Thou* has a different basis . . .
> When *Thou* is spoken, the speaker has no *thing*; he has indeed nothing. But he takes his stand in relation. [63]

> As EXPERIENCE the world belongs to the primary word *I-It*.
> The primary word *I-Thou* establishes the world of RELATION. [64]

> The history of the individual and that of the human race indicate a progressive augmentation of the world of *It*. [65]

> The primary connexion of man with the world of *It* is comprised in *experiencing* and *using* . . . [66]

> We only need to fill each moment with experiencing using, and it ceases to burn. [67]

> If I face a human being as my *Thou*, and say the primary word *I-Thou* to him, he is not a thing among things, and does not consist of things.
> Thus human being is not *He* or *She*, bounded from every other *He* and *She*, a specific point in space and time within the net of the world; nor is he a nature able to be experienced and described, a loose bundle of named qualities. But with no neighbour, and whole in himself, he

is *Thou* and fills the heavens. This does not mean that nothing exists except himself. But all else lives in *his* light. [68]

Where any of this leads us, how one gets there — these are, as I have said, the province of other chapters. But by looking closely here at just what Buber has done, we may avoid misunderstandings and at the same time familiarize ourselves with those essential features of neo-Hasidism that will be helpful in our readings of the novels.

In the deceptively simple expressions such as those I have cited, Buber moves in on the modern problem and devours it. He is not only saying that the civilization of science and technology has turned us into objects and objectifiers, alone and unhappy — but he is saying *how* science and technology have done this; and, more than that, he is saying, as did Kierkegaard, that the *only* solution rests in our ability to reidentify with the sacred.

With a powerful brevity that is itself a mystery, Buber's words have this to tell us: When we lost the ability to respond to the supersensible, two pretenders to the throne won our ultimate attention, won the kingdom, the power, and the glory, These gods are Science (God as Limit or Control) and Technology (God as Machine). We *are* alone, we *are* alienated, and the reason is that the twin gods of the mechano-technical age are the powers with which we identify. Our prayers are the saying of *It*. "M-machinery'll make an ocean of commodities," Robey, the stuttering philosopher, tells Augie March. "Dictators can't stop it. Man will accept death. Live without God. That's a b-brave project. End of an illusion. But with what values instead. . . . But that [says Robey, says Bellow, says Buber] that's toward the end of the book." [69]

When we identify with the God of Science, when we conclude, for example, that spirit or love are limited in the same way as matter — neither created nor destroyed — then we surrender what is holy about our humanness, we surrender the *Thou*, and take our place in the world of things.

"Science," writes W. Macneile Dixon, "is of intention inhuman, supposing, strange as it may seem, that the further we travel from ourselves the nearer we approach the truth." [70]

When we identify with the God of Technology, when we

either give to the machine a holiness we deny ourselves (as in our terror and wonder for the computer) or make of ourselves a machine unhallowed, denying again our holiness, then we again surrender the *Thou*, and take our place in the world of things. "In the hopes and fears of the machine age," Bruno Bettelheim writes, "savior and destroyer are no longer clothed in the image of man; no longer are the figures that we imagine can save and destroy us direct projections of our human experience. What we now hope will save us, and what in our delusions we fear will destroy us, is something that no longer has human qualities — that device or projection is the machine."[71]

But "man cannot approach the divine," Buber writes, "by reaching beyond the human," whether that be to some theological God apart from men and women or to some *machina ex deus*. Instead, we are called to the primary word, the saying of Thou, in and to ourselves. *Sh'ma Yisrael, hear O Israel*. This morning's cantor, Allen Ginsberg:

> In the midst of the broken consciousness of mid twentieth century suffering and anguish of separation from my own body and its natural infinity of feeling its own self one with all self, I instinctively seeking to reconstitute that blissful union which I experienced so rarely I took it to be supernatural and gave it holy Name thus made it hymn laments of longing and litanies of triumphancy of Self over the mind illusion mechano-universe of unfeeling Time in which I saw my self my own mother and my very nation trapped desolate our worlds of consciousness homeless and at war. . . . These poems almost un-conscious to confess the beatific human fact . . . the self seeking the Key to life found at last in our self.[72]

But in pointing to the threat of technology and science Buber does not do what so many have done in his name: He does not condemn the machine, nor does he condemn reason. Although the machine, he says, should not be made a god, although, as Thoreau warned, we must not become the tools of our tools, still, using the same language, Buber quotes the Ba'al Shem: "One should have mercy on the holy sparks."[73] There are sacred possibilities for our technology as well. What we must do, Buber seems to be saying, is not eliminate machines, but eliminate our identification with the machine, our identification with use and manipulation. (Does this turn you on, turn you off, switch you on, blow your mind — or are you perhaps not programmed to give me feedback on my input?) Things simply, like the profane, are not to be abandoned but redeemed: "All things wait to be hallowed by man."[74]

Nor does Buber decry the scientific. He does not call us away from rationality, law, limit, or control, but away from identifying our own spirit with any of these. As the *zaddikim* have written, "Infinity shall be contained in every deed of man."

Neo-Hasidism professes that what is needed is not less science nor less technology, but more identification with the sacred, with the world and self as sacred, with the spaces in relation where the sacred is brought to life. These very distinctions — in order for us to accept the Law of the Conservation of Energy without denying the power of the heart to create and destroy, in order to accept the computer as wonderful without denying the wonder in ourselves — require the powers of reason.[75]

Neo-Hasidism, then, in the best tradition of its antecedent, makes the claim that mysticism can be reasonable. The significance this has for the work of Malamud and Bellow will be felt directly in our reading of the novels. In one way or another all of the protagonists are like Yakov Bok, who, riding out of the *shtetl*, carries with him the mystery of the *tefillin*, itself reasonable, and the reason of Spinoza, itself mysterious. But what better image of the reasonable and the mystical intertwined than the matter to which we are moving: Art itself is mystery. Art — immeasurable yet infused with reason; art — without limit and yet controlled: Art is the mystery wrought by man. "Forget this," as e.e. cummings says, "and you will have forgotten the mystery which you have been, the mystery which you shall be, and the mystery which you are."[76]

All art is a mystery, and the affirmative novel doubly so: a mystery through form and a mystery through content. In tracing the literary and philosophic personality of our century we found ourselves wandering in the desert. We indicated that the twentieth-century philosophy of neo-Hasidism, having moved through the same spaces as its contemporaries, moves, by mystery, beyond deserting toward a human home. Finally it is promised that, like the visions that preceded it, accompanying voices in the American novel can begin to be heard. "Bellow's celebration of the temporary world," Keith Michael Opdahl observes, "his emphasis on community and love, and his rejection of the formal for the spontaneous and individual all unite his fiction with Hasidism, his love of the particular scene or event at the expense of larger form, conveying the sense that the particular may contain the larger mystery, may owe something not only to the Romantics but to the faith and the anecdotal, aphoristic literature of the Hasids."[77] "It remains to be asked," writes Chester Eisenger, first to mention the thesis at hand, "what are the literary consequences of the Hasidic temperament?"[78] The question still remains. We ask it now and hope to give it answer in the chapters that follow.

But just as it is important to place neo-mysticism in relation to the Hasidic thought from which it derives, so it is important to indicate similar debts with respect to the immediate *literary* antecedents for the affirmative novel. It would be misleading to leave our portrayal of the century's literary personality devoid of *any* connection to the mystery Buber implies when he says that "God can be beheld in each thing and in each pure deed." One thinks, for example, of the work of Herman Hesse, Nikos Kazantzakis, James Joyce, D. H. Lawrence.

Joyce's *Ulysses,* as Barrett writes, "breaks with the whole tradition of Western sensibility and Western aesthetics in showing each small object of Bloom's day — even the objects in his pocket, like a cake of soap — as capable at certain moments of taking on a transcendental importance. Each grain of sand, Joyce seems to be saying, reflects the whole universe."[79] "God," Joyce wrote, "is a shout in the streets."

But more than anyone — and it is odd, for the man has rarely been linked with Joyce — Lawrence provides the passion and principle from which the affirmative novel has grown.

All that Lawrence wrote throbbed with the pulse of his "circumambient universe." He is a prototype for the neo-mystic: inveighing against passionless rationality, urging

us on to make contact with the inner darkness and the outer
vibration — yet all along, getting it down, shaping the words,
controlling the experience, being the artist.

Statement and definition (of great use to us) emerge through
the bravura of Lawrence's criticism, unknowingly announcing
Buber to literature. But before this, it would be good to look at
Lawrence the novelist, where Hasidic and neo-Hasidic tradition are not announced but lived:

> They felt the rush of the sap in spring, they knew the
> wave which cannot halt, but every year throws forward
> the seed to begetting, and falling back, leaves the young
> born on the earth. They knew the intercourse between
> heaven and earth, sunshine drawn into the breast and
> bowels, the rain sucked up in the daytime, nakedness that
> comes under the wind in autumn, showing the birds' nests
> no longer worth hiding. Their life and interrelations were
> such; feeling the pulse and body of the soil, that opened
> to their furrow for the grain, and became smooth and
> supple after their ploughing, and clung to their feet with a
> weight that pulled like desire, lying hard and unrespon-
> sive when the crops were to be shorn away. The young
> corn waved and was silken, and the lustre slid along the
> limbs of the men who saw it. They took the udder of the
> cows; the cows yielded milk and pulse against the hands
> of the men, the pulse of the blood of the teats of the cows
> beat into the pulse of the hands of the men . . . [80]

So human being was in its first generation — at one with the
universe, holy in Eden, unborn to awareness, eternally *Thou*.
The pot of gold is merely given — is a part of being — at the
beginning of *The Rainbow*. The spirit and content of the passage remind us of the Hasidic folktale: "The legends of
Hasids," Buber says, "tell much of these wonderful
men . . . who looked from one end of the earth to the other,
and saw all changes which happened in the world and who
were as much aware of them as though they occurred in their
own body." [81] Lawrence's story shows the men and women of
ensuing generations, fallen from grace, human being as we
know it, as Buber knows it: moving together and moving apart,
facing a person and facing a thing, fighting the mind,
battling *It*, reaching a *Thou*, dying again. Through the

changing rainbow of the Brangwens' relationships, Lawrence's prose pushes the reader and pulls him away, carries his body through the rhythms of life, physically shows him what Buber means by "Without *It* man cannot live. But he who lives with *It* alone is not a man — is not a man." [82] These are the rhythms, this is the rocking in reading the novels of Bellow and Malamud.

Lawrence's *Studies in Classic American Literature* provide us with a useful and important vocabulary for speaking about novels driven by and connected to the mystery he understands so well. [83] The essential function of art, Lawrence tells us, is not aesthetic, but moral. Morality, however, is no fixed or absolute idea. It is instead, for Lawrence, an instinct for life, a sympathy for the state of one's inner and outer relatedness. We have inner wholeness (or outer wholeness) when we are bigger than the sum of our parts in relation to ourselves (or to the universe). It is the essential function of the novel to connect the individual with the mystery that makes him or her greater than the sum of his or her parts. The novel can do this — and only the novel, Lawrence says — by being moral, by awaking us to the fluidity of relationship: the sense of an ever-changing balance between the person and his or her cir-cumambient universe. This is the sort of morality Buber under-stands when he says, "The mystical soul cannot become real if it is not one with the moral." [84] This is the sort of morality Bellow had in mind, I believe, when he wrote Opdahl that his "intention has remained intensely moral." [85] This is the sort of morality to which Sidney Richman really refers when he senses Malamud's literary struggle is "a moral struggle — an effort to escape contemporary limitations and rejoin the prophetic vision." [86]

We turn now to those novels of Malamud and Bellow that are, above all, moral as Lawrence defines the word: they deal with our movements toward inner and outer wholeness, with the person becoming bigger than the sum of his parts. Augie, Herzog, and Henderson, Yakov Bok and Frank Alpine — all seek and become, through their inner and outer relatedness, bigger, much bigger than the sum of their parts: "I am not," says Alpine, "the same guy I was."[87] "Oh you . . . Some-thing," Henderson cries out in the jungle, "You Something because of whom there is not Nothing." [88]

"I saw human life," Buber writes, "as a dialogue with being."

This is the sweeter end to alienation. Many critics have sensed some kind of an end to the chronicle by and of the modern man adrift. They trumpet in "The novel of accommodation" as a finish to our dark night of the soul. But this will not do. The accommodationists see the turn of the novel as the result of exhaustion from the terrors of nihilism. "Despite the hatred in everyone," writes Marcus Klein, "despite violence, despite weakness and sickness, despite the uncertainty of ordinary reality, despite everything, the human community is possible."[89] And this is so: the human community *is* possible; but it is not possible merely because the aforesaid horrors are too tiring to dwell on — the human community is not possible merely because, as Klein says, it is "plainly necessary" that it be possible.[90] "Over against all this behavior of present day man," Buber, it seems, should say again, "Hasidism sets the simple truth that the wretchedness of our world is grounded in its resistance to the entrance of the holy into lived life."

That the holy *is* there in the human community is the reason the human community is possible. And that the holy is *not* there in Klein's reading of Malamud and Bellow is the reason why his words about the novels do not satisfy, do not seem to go nearly as far as the fiction itself. Klein hears the authors saying that merely out of necessity we must accommodate, we must adjust to "the ordinary, the domestic, the painfully contingent" — and in our adjusting find love there.[91] But Malamud and Bellow, like Buber before them, are not talking about accommodation: One does not accommodate the holy. "I love the old bitch just the way she is," Henderson says of the world, "and I like to think I am always prepared for even the very worst she has to show me. I am a true adorer of life, and if I can't reach as high as the face of it, I plant my kiss somewhere lower down."[92] The hallowing of the everyday is not a turning away but a turning toward — and the love that we find there, like the love we find in Buber, Bellow, and Malamud, is not love that is merely happened upon in turning away (of which we are no longer embarrassed to speak), but love to which we are driven, sensing as we do that it may answer ultimate needs and call from us ultimate answers. Bound up in it we are bigger than the sum of our parts, "in love" in some way of which we are perhaps properly embarrassed to speak.

Bigger than the sum of our parts: and so we return to the mystery: of human being, through will and grace, saying *Thou* to that part no longer a part.

Bigger than the sum of its parts: and so we return to the mystery: of art, controlled yet immeasurable, ordered yet alive, shaped by reason and yet true.

As life is created by the divine, so art is created by the divine in man. The works of God and man are a mystery, immeasurable — but not unapproachable. We move to them and are moved by them. We do not seek to measure but to hallow. And our criticism — of life and of art — should be the saying of *Thou*.

farbrengen *

On an airplane the Hasidic rabbi who invited us to live in Crown Heights is hoping there will be no delay in landing. In this is he any different from the cost accountant on his left? There are schedules that must be kept. The rabbi's is tied to the change of the light, to the turning of the earth. This cannot be altered. If there is no delay he will be able to pray the afternoon service in some privacy.

The captain's voice announces that they are over the city on time, but there are several planes that must land ahead of them. They will circle above until it is their turn to land, after which they will be guided by radar through the dense cloud layer below.

The rabbi shrugs and makes ready to pray the afternoon service. He gets out his prayer book. While he walks to the back of the plane he ties a rope around his middle to separate the lower half of his body from the higher half. In the back of the cabin, amidst the magazine racks and the lavatory doors, he tries to figure out which way east is. This amuses him. They were heading east, but now that they are circling it is a complicated affair.

---

*The farbrengen, literally a gathering, usually comes as a refresher between more strenuous periods of study or prayer on the Sabbath or special holidays. The heart of the gathering, of course, is the rebbe's tales, which, relating in one form or another to the Torah portion the community has read together earlier, become a model of literary criticism, telling stories to stories. The relationship of the tales themselves, each to the other, is seldom apparent as the tales unfold. But by the end of the farbrengen a whole usually emerges, the gathering a matter not of getting there, but of staying.

In the chapters themselves, I occasionally tell a tale I heard while I lived with the Hasidim. In the farbrengen I am trying to say something of the tales I saw.

Soon after he begins praying a bell is sounded in the cabin. While he is saying the fourteen blessings, bending and bowing at the name of the Lord, a stewardess in a pantsuit comes to tell him that he must take his seat now as they are coming down to land.

He nods agreeably, but does not speak. These are silent blessings. She leaves while a voice from the speakers says it is an FAA regulation that seatbacks be moved forward to a full upright position. Outside it is white. They are in the middle of heavy clouds.

He takes three steps forward and three steps back, bowing before a holy throne. He is mumbling, hurrying, but concentrating. He is close to finishing. He has regulations, too. The stewardess returns. She is alarmed, embarrassed. She stands by him, sees he is busy in some way that revolts and intrigues her. But more important, he is a passenger standing in the cabin of an airplane on final approach! "Sir, you must go to your seat immediately." He nods but continues, rocking slightly. "We're going to land any minute!" Nothing. "We're just about to break through!"

The rabbi smiles at her reassuringly. "So am I," he says.

THE ASSISTANT'S SERVICE

It was, in the night, as though I had been faced by my own reflection in the depths of a somber and immense mirror. [1]
— Joseph Conrad,
"The Secret Sharer"

No matter where and when you meet him you feel that he has come from some place — no matter from what place he has come — some country that he has devoured rather than resided in, some secret land that he has been nourished on but cannot inherit, for the Jew seems to be everywhere from nowhere. [2]
— Djuna Barnes,
Nightwood

Today I'm as ancient in years as the Jewish people themselves are. It seems to me at this moment — I am an Israelite. [3]
— Yevgeny Yevtushenko,
"Babii Yar"

The Assistant mixes the flavor of the Hasidic folktale with the fervor of the twentieth-century quest. The result is startling. Malamud, a *macher* indeed, fashions Identity itself, alive and dancing, and in so doing, brings to life the very rhythm of the *I-Thou* relationship — a self-transcending communication. Mystery abounds, redounds to the reader: life is renewed, creation continuous. *The Assistant* is, in greatest part, of a cool or stern mysticism — as characteristic of

Malamud's mystery as heat and explosion are proper to Bellow —of a stern mysticism, to be likened to the Hasidic stance of *aboda*, of service or devotion, of "collecting oneself and becoming at one."[4] Akin to this is the notion of the *yihud,* the unity of the transcendent — that a man produces or creates the unity of the transcendent through the unity of his own becoming.[5] The man of becoming, this Frank Alpine, comes out of nowhere, the American man, belonging to nothing, lastly himself, rightly defined by what he is not ("a goy after all"[6]), a man wholly disjoint. "What am I," *aboda* asks, "and what is my life?"[7]

Alpine's identity is the central concern of even our first meeting with him when he comes into the store. It is our concern: he is masked, a white handkerchief over his face (p. 24). It is his concern: "A cracked mirror hung behind him on the wall above the sink and every so often he turned to stare into it." (p. 24). And it is Morris's concern: the grocer's "frightened eyes sought the man's but he was looking elsewhere" (p. 24).

Looking elsewhere or not, the grocer and the robber, at this first meeting, experience an oddly primal sort of communication as the two men take water from the same cup (p. 24); and so, in this folktale fashion of his, Malamud introduces the spirit of the *yihud* through the act of meeting, the act of union; Malamud lets us know that whoever this man is he is going to relate to Morris in a way that runs deep, to the core, to the beginning.

Through the flavor of folktale Malamud manages — without any damage to the story — to pull across every page the continuing question, "Who is this Frank Alpine?" We know at the start, from the intensity of their unity, that the answer lies in Morris Bober; and Alpine himself — as in need of the answer as the rest of us, the man of becoming, of *aboda,* mystically attached to Morris — repeatedly emerges as the grocer's savior. *Aboda* is service: "all action bound in one and the infinite carried into every action: this is *aboda.*"[8] Frank's repeated saving of Morris has about it the mystery of something bigger than persons. It is that which exists *between* persons: it is relationship. It is here, say Buber and Malamud — each in his own way — it is here that the sacred resides.

Saving the grocer the first time wins Alpine legitimate entry to the house where he is at once a stranger — this disciple of St. Francis, this "Italyener," this man who when eating a Jewish roll says, "Jesus, this is hard bread" (p. 27) — and at once a familiar — "Morris knew a poor man when he saw one" (p. 30), being a poor man himself. Alpine evokes in the grocer a sense of repulsion — "He shifted in his chair, fearing to catch some illness" (p. 31), and a sense of affinity — "I am sixty, he talks like me" (p. 33), and throughout this first face-to-meeting the two men continue to communicate on an order as primal and pure as the sharing of water:

> Why don't he go home, Morris thought.
> "I'm going," Frank said (p. 33).

But *The Assistant* is not a folktale or a myth. It is not, like Malamud's first novel, *The Natural*, a story of magic through and through. Instead Malamud waits until the reader is drawn into a real frame before he begins without warning to distort that frame. Malamud creates a real frame by giving us perfectly plausible motives for Frank's appearance and desire to remain in the store: at first we see this as guilt at his thievery and pity for Morris; and then, when this wears thin, the author introduces the attraction to Helen, Morris's daughter. Malamud draws us into the frame by duping us twice over: by the promise of superior knowledge, and by a pretense to gimmickry. We think we know more than Morris and Helen. But this is of course a deception. The reason Frank stays *is* because of Morris and Helen, but only initially for the reasons we suppose. There is a force growing here, about which we have no knowledge whatever, and when we do begin finally to sense that this is so, when the frame of reality begins to give way, it is too late. We are caught.

We know before anyone, for example, that Frank is the man who robbed the store. Thus Helen's feeling that Frank "had done something — had committed himself in a way she couldn't guess" (p. 97) is quickly understood by us to refer to the robbery. It is only later that — duped into thinking we know all the dynamics — thoroughly drawn into the store and the story — we discover the exact nature of Frank's commitment: to learn self, to learn relation. In the same way, Malamud is careful to inform the reader that Frank's touching self-explorations before the grocer are little more than theater.

When Frank says to Morris, "Something is missing in me," Malamud follows this with "Frank felt he had all he wanted from him at the moment" (p. 34). This is, at the moment, convincing enough for us. We feel we understand the man and his motives.

Dwelling in what we think is a completely real world we see Frank's move toward Jewishness as the author's device to indicate the development of Frank's relationship to Helen and Morris. We think of the emerging identity as significant in terms of its sameness to that of Helen and Morris. In other words, if we are thinking about it, we think of it as a gimmick. In fact, however, as we come to learn in what is the essential experience of the story, the move toward Jewishness is the very definition of these relationships. For example, in the beginning, when we see Alpine dressed in the grocer's clothes, then stripped of them, then in them again more firmly than before, we feel that with the subtlety of a small hammer Malamud is saying, "Look, Frank is becoming like Morris." Exposed to this kind of surface work, we feel we are simply being *told* he is getting more Jewish rather than being *shown* what it *is* to be Jewish and so we think of Jewishness as an indicator, a device.

Unthreatened by obvious device, made comfortable by prior knowledge, we are relaxed in a situation we are convinced we understand. There seems to be nothing going on that is beyond our control: a reader likes this feeling of sitting on high, looking down and deciding it's all very interesting. And Malamud makes certain we stay convinced of our superiority. If we were thinking some deeper attraction might be involved, and had begun to ask ourselves, "What exactly can Frank get from Morris?", Malamud quiets this thought in Bober's line that, swallowed here, becomes difficult to digest later on: "What can you learn here? Only one thing — heartache" (p.35). If and when we are no longer satisfied that Alpine remains at the store simply out of guilt or pity, when we are on the verge of discovering with what kind of energies we are really dealing, Malamud feeds us a little more line by introducing the second motive — the attraction to Helen. Fine. This we understand. The fish stays and the hook is set.

Now that he has us Malamud spares us nothing. The mere wearing of the Jew's apron, and "the clean clothes Morris had sent down [for Alpine] that fitted him after Ida lengthened and pressed the cuffs" (p. 48) — all of this easy role-playing, this telling, gives way to internal wrenching, internal lengthening and pressing. Guilt at his deed, lust for the daughter — hah! — this is just the sort of tolerable anguish to pull Frank and the reader into the house. What is he doing there? He answers the question — significantly enough — with a question of his own: "What is the Jew," he asks, "to me?" (p. 58). And what are *we* doing there? Why, we hardly know. Only a moment before everything seemed so clear. The story was being told to us, and now — now it's hard to explain, things have a new shape, or rather no shape at all. And there we are, with Frank, in the middle of things, looking for something we can recognize. It is the most difficult task of all for a twentieth-century American author to bring his reader to transcendent mystery. Yet this is, as he has told me, Malamud's very goal. "My job" he has said, "is to create mystery. Exemplification of mystery is the creation of mystery."[9] And if it can only be done by a trick, then at least it can still be done. Saul Bellow, as we will see, accomplished the end through the American voice in *Augie March* and through myth in *Henderson the Rain King*. Malamud, in *The Fixer*, pretends to historical perspective. In *The Assistant* he dupes us by setting up a frame of reality that we can objectify, and then distorting that reality, disturbing our peace, toppling us into the story itself, never telling us anything again, passing all of it on through relation:

> What kind of a man did you have to be to shut yourself up in an overgrown coffin? You had to be a Jew. They were born prisoners. Deadly patience, endurance. That's what they live for, Frank thought, to suffer. And the one that has got the biggest pain in the gut and can hold onto it the longest without running to the toilet is the best Jew. No wonder they got on his nerves! (pp. 70 - 71).

Patience and endurance get on his nerves. Yet he is drawn, violently, desperately, to the two people who represent these qualities to him. For Helen, too, repeatedly alarms him with her "determination" and her "seriousness" (p.95). Their relationship, like that with Morris, is clearly shaped by Alpine's drive to find some shape of his own.

And though there is an important distinction, which we will discuss later, it is as much through Helen as Morris that we see the identity emerging. Through Helen, too, we are in the presence of *aboda*, of a special service whose purpose is to answer the question "Who am I and what is my life?" As their relationship tightens Alpine grows enough for Helen to sense, if only subconsciously, that her confusion — "something evasive about him, something hidden. . . . He sometimes appeared to be more than he was, sometimes less" — that this confusion has a name: "Don't forget," she blurts uncontrollably, "I'm Jewish" (pp.96 - 97). He replies, "So what?" and thinks of himself as crashing through a wall. A commitment is made and it is followed by the desire for instruction. "What do Jews believe in?" he asks Morris. And though he has not yet grown enough to appreciate how profound is his instructor, he is faced with the most essential definition of Jewishness Malamud or Hasidism are able to impart:

> "Why do they suffer so much? It seems they like to suffer."
> "They suffer because they are Jews."
> "More than they have to?"
> "If you live you suffer."
> "What do you suffer for, Morris?"
> "For you."
> "What do you mean?"
> "I mean you suffer for me" (p. 98).

Here is the core of the novel. It is to this moment that all action real and mystical has led; and it is from this moment that all action real and mystical proceeds. We have learned by this time that Frank's metamorphosis is something more than a gimmick, that we are involved with definition; but not until this moment are we given that definition. We have seen the mystery of *aboda* and *yihud* in the repeated rescuing of Morris, in the strange way the two men are drawn together; and we will see it again in Frank's later "discipline," in the "unity of becoming" that is the story's climax — but the essential Hasidic mystery, the mystery the Hasidim saved from Judaism, and that Buber consecrated into the *I-Thou* relationship, is the mystery to be found in these lines:

> "What do you suffer for, Morris?"
> "For you."
> "What do you mean?"

"I mean you suffer for me."

The first words of Hasidism, the spoken tale, which Buber says "developed out of a simple necessity to create a verbal expression adequate to an overpowering objective reality," which have, "at their base . . . the stammering of inspired witnesses"[10] record the mystery Malamud exhumes in the dialogue above. The Hasidim tell the story of Rabbi Aaron of Karlin, who, desiring to greet a friend a long way from his home, set out one day to reach him. After a long trip he found his door, knocked on it, and heard a voice say, "Who is it?" Rabbi Aaron answered, "I," and was refused admission. Returning to his home, Rabbi Aaron spent a year grieving and considering what had passed. At the end of this time he set out again for the home of his friend. Again he knocked on the door, and again he heard a voice within say, "Who is it?" This time Rabbi Aaron answered, "Thou" and was admitted. [11]

But inasmuch as Frank does not understand Morris, is not at this stage ready to understand, let us ourselves grow with him into the shape of this mystery. Frank has some distance to travel. While there is certainly truth to his repeated phrase "I am not the same guy I was," he has only glimpsed the significance of what Malamud chooses to call "discipline." That he has none himself he demonstrates twice over by trying to rob what he needs to complete himself from the two people he knows to possess it. But what he needs from the grocer is not money, nor from the daughter, sex. What he needs are not things. He emerges at this stage a Jew only to the undiscerning eye of Ward Minogue ("You stinking kike" [p. 115]), whose misperception is grotesquely underscored by the donation of his identity to Alpine himself, a man that night as far from the covenant as any man might be — "Dog, uncircumcised dog," Helen yells at him after he violates her (p.131). "The span of a man's life lies between seeking and finding," Buber says of *aboda.* "Yea, a thousand-fold backsliding of the weak and wandering soul." [12]

Frank is a man in search of fulfillment. He is in need. In robbing Morris of his money, Helen of her virginity, he seeks perversely to satisfy that need, demonstrating its intensity. "He spoke of his starved and passionate love, and all the endless heartbreaking waiting. Even as he spoke he thought of her as beyond his reach . . ." (p.133). But Frank is the man of *aboda,* of service, the assistant. This is his way to fulfillment. In the language of neo-Hasidism, it is only through achieving the relationship of an *I* to a *Thou* with Morris and Helen, rather than treating them as things, or uses, that he will reach such fulfillment. Although the relationship to Helen is different from the one with Morris — the first within the frame of reality, the second, allegorical, and beyond it — Frank serves each, is devoted to each, and his fate rests upon what he can learn from the first to apply to the second.

Only now, wallowing in self-disgust, does Frank learn that he has within him the muscle for discipline, for self-initiated devotion, for *aboda*: "He discovered that all the while he was acting like he wasn't he was really a man of stern morality" (p.139). Once again he saves the grocer, who this time has nearly asphyxiated himself; but this kind of service we have seen before. It is part of the mystical wave that washes over the story. Frank must do it himself, unassisted either by Nick, the other tenant, or forces beyond himself: "He would do it all on his own will, nobody pushing him but himself" (p.145).

Now Frank's service becomes mysterious. Though bound ever more intensely to the grocer he becomes himself the object of his assistance, and to more than either of them, it is to an ultimate focus — the relationship *between*, the holy sparks seeking redemption — that he is drawn. We have wondered throughout at Frank's *intentions;* now suddenly the matter is transformed, suffused by Forster's "bar of light." Frank's intentions have become "*kavanas*," the mystery of the intending soul directed to redemption, goalful, but without purpose. *Kavana* is not will," Buber writes:

> It does not think of transplanting an image into the world of actual things, of making fast a dream as an object so that it may be at hand, to be experienced at one's convenience in satiating recurrence. Nor does it desire to throw the stone of action into the well of happening that its waters may for a while become troubled and astonished, only to return then to the deep command of their existence . . . not this is *kavana's* meaning, that the horses pulling the great wagon should feel one impulse more or that one building more should be erected beneath the awe-full gaze of the stars. *Kavana* does not mean purpose but goal.[13]

But this is difficult for the purposeful assistant to learn. In his frenzied rededication to fulfill himself he reads a history of the Jews, "trying to figure out why they are the Chosen People," (p.151); but he cannot. "But," Buber writes of *kavana,*

> the liberation [of the holy sparks, the redemption from the exile within] does not take place through formulae of exorcism or through any kind of prescribed and special action. All this grows out of the ground of otherness, which is not the ground of *kavana.* No leap from the everyday into the miraculous is required. . . . It is not the matter of the action, but only its dedication that is decisive. Just that which you do in the uniformity of recurrence or in the disposition of events, just this answer of the acting person to the manifold demands of the hour — an answer acquired through practice or won through inspiration — just this continuity of the living stream, when accomplished in dedication, leads to redemption.[14]

Frank works. He works twenty hours a day, giving all of his money, all of himself, to the Bober family. He cleans the store, repaints the walls, varnishes the shelves. He suffers, he repents, he waits, and keeps serving: "All action bound in one,"[15] doing it, "with discipline and with love" (p. 145). It is a period of ultimate service: "Frank felt he would promise anything to stay there" (p. 145). There is in his devotion, in *aboda* with *kavana,* the quality of prayer, of prayer as the Hasidim understand it: "Men think they pray before God, but it is not so, for prayer itself is divinity." [16]

In Frank's final rescue of Morris from the fire, Frank is able himself, beyond the mystical wave that seems to keep bringing them together, to see the necessity of their union, of their meeting. His language indicates that he does not yet understand exactly how the union is effected; still he says it: "For Christ's sake, Morris, take me back here" (p.186). "Each act becomes divine service and divine work when it is directed toward the union." [17]

But that union is not finally consummated — cannot be consummated — until Morris dies, dies as he lived, brushing away a little snow, which, before his body is cold, returns to fill in the little space he cleared. As the relationship between

Morris and Frank has been carried out beyond the reality frame, as they are, in relation, not so much persons as the personification of the *I-Thou* relationship itself, Frank's at-one-ment becomes a celebrative collecting of Morris.

The ultimate act of Alpine's conversion, the complete coming together, is a story painted with the color and stroke of the Hasidic folktale. In its brightness and fancy, joy and sadness it most vividly calls to mind the work of Marc Chagall. Pushed by that wave that moves over the entire story, Alpine falls into his teacher's grave, "flailing his arms, landing feet first," "dancing," as Helen and Ida see it, "on the grocer's coffin" (p.182). In this moment Alpine receives the one gift the grocer has to give — his identity — as the *I-Thou* relationship is literally consummated. Here the transcendent is most powerfully present through the metaphorical acting out of the notion of the *yihud:* one produces or creates the unity of God through the unity of his own becoming.

In fulfillment *aboda* is transcended and replaced by ecstasy: "*Hitlahabut* is as far from *aboda* as fulfillment is from longing. And yet *hitlahabut* streams out of *aboda* as the finding of God from the seeking of God. . . . As *aboda* flows out to *hitlahabut*, the basic principle of Hasidic life, so here too *kavana* flows into *hitlahabut*. . . . He who serves in perfection . . . [brings] . . . *hitlahabut* into the heart of *aboda*. He who has ascended from *aboda* to *hitlahabut* has submerged his will in service, and receives his deed from it alone, having risen above every separate service.[18] In this moment Frank Alpine is prayer. Of *hitlahabut*, Buber has written: "At times it reveals itself in some action which it consecrates and fills with holy significance. The purest manifestation is in *dance*. In this the whole body becomes subservient to the ecstatic soul. Out of a thousand waves of movement it evokes in a kindred and visible form an image of the many fluctuations of elation and dejection of the enraptured soul. 'Among all who saw his holy dancing, there was not one in whom a divine conversion did not take place.' . . . "[19]

This is the moment of Alpine's conversion, the complete unification: "all walls have fallen, all boundary stones are uprooted, all separation is destroyed," as Buber says it.[20] Only a moment before dancing in the grave, while sitting in the synagogue, he was not a Jew. He thought then, "Suffering to them is like a piece of goods. I bet the Jews could make a suit of clothes out of it" (p.181). But a moment after having left the grave, suffering is not to him a thing, something to be worn or traded. But instead it is something within which one effects the most essential sort of communication: "He felt pity on the world for harboring him" (p.182). He expresses his suffering for himself in terms of his suffering for that which is beyond himself. Woven into his expression of feeling for another is the apprehension of the other's feeling for him. He both eliminates himself and increases himself as he himself becomes no part and all part of relationship.

He is the Jew. He is Morris. The women in the family think of him not as the clerk but as "the grocer." His hair, like Morris's has grown thick. He is attached, with the same irony, to the Yiddish newspaper *The Forward*. And keenest of all, for no reason he has to explain, he finds himself awaking to get the Polisheh her three cents' worth of rolls. Of that practice he had said earlier, "Who but a Jew?"

> "What do you suffer for, Morris?"
> "For you."
> "What do you mean?"
> "I mean you suffer for me."

Within the Hasidic context Malamud brings to life the mystery of two men relating so perfectly that one person becomes that other person to whom he relates. The pure and perfect communication that takes place in the beginning of the book, when the two men share water, finds its mystically mature expression in Frank's actual assumption of Morris's identity.

But Malamud's mysticism has been carefully confined to Alpine's relationship with the grocer. The lesson we learn here — in a world removed from our own — is important only as we see it can be applied to the world we understand; only Frank is person as well as metaphor. The author is careful to screen the relationship with Helen from any of these flights from the frame of reality. It is here, in the real-life situation, that the lesson is applied. "Love," Buber tells us, "is the responsibility of an *I* for a *Thou*." [21] We have learned through the personification of an idea that the essence of the relationship is a responsibility — an ability to respond — that results in one person becoming the other. Is there a sense in which we see this to happen in realistic terms between Frank and Helen? Both Frank and Helen want a college education more than anything else, yet at the book's end each expresses this desire in terms of providing the college education for the other.

Nonetheless, in characteristic fashion, Malamud gives us only a hopeful indication that the young people will be able to achieve such a relationship. Moses, Morris, the book itself — they wander through the desert and die with salvation still left to be written . . . by the reader.

What Malamud has written for us is the wandering, the moving to the edge. And he has written it in the form of a painstakingly slow moment-by-moment account of one person relating to another man. Who is the other? He is a man who has been in the desert all his life. When he tells Morris of his life (and Morris tells him of the Old Country) he tells tales of "wandering" and "long periods of travel." He is the man born in the wilderness: "Now all of the people that came out were circumcised; but all the people that were born in the wilderness by the way as they came forth out of Egypt, them they had not circumcised" (Joshua 5:3). Born in this country of Italian origin, an orphan for as long as he can remember — cut loose from father and fatherland — he is from every part of the United States and from no part. He is the American.

Malamud really carries one step further Joyce's story of Leopold Bloom, the wandering Jew of the modern world. Having lost his son while still a child, left only with a daughter, Bloom is reunited at the end of his day to the father-son relationship, as he and Stephen — so promising yet so in need of father and friend — share cocoa in the early hours of the morning. In effect, what Malamud has done with Morris and Frank is to nurture the seed that seems to have been planted amidst the fertile energy of Molly Bloom's closing soliloquy. Rudy has returned. As Buber has said: "Every man can say *Thou* and is then *I*, every man can say Father and is then Son." [22]

farbrengen

Rifka told me right away she was no Hasid. "This *you could know from the Super Duper,"* she said.
This I did not understand.

We had been talking, as usual with Rifka, about several things at once — Hasids, why she was so exhausted today, children. There was a story coming. How could she be a Hasid if she would buy, in a pinch, from a store that was not kosher?

"I vhass at the Super Duper Food Store. Les' night came home the whole family, my boys, vhat are avay at collitch, and my daughter vit her husband that doesn't verk God should bless him. So, I am making for my Harold like he likes it kreplach to eat. And vit it, for my Louis that came home for the veekend vit a girl, nuch, a matza ball soup vit schmaltz. And vhat should happen — I need the aggravation — there is no schmaltz. I got a housefulla guests, a fency girl from Scarsdale vhat my Louis brings home and — my mazel — no schmaltz."

At this I smile and Rifka frowns at me.

"So. I go to the Super Duper. I'm hurrying to get back to my dinner I valk through the aisle I see her. I saw a voman vit her child vhat vhass an idiot. You could see he vhass an idiot. I saw this voman, I saw this mother, she vas holding two different kinds mustard. I vhass in a hurry. I had my schmaltz and I vent out of the store.

"That night vhen all my children and guests vere asleep I vhass not. I could not. I could not go asleep. Vhy? I din't know. I vhass thinking of all the excitement and it vhass hot but I could not go asleep.

"And then vitout — I mean I din't do it myself, I started to cry. And I cried. I cried for that mother vit her idiot vhat kept on living. I cried for that mother vhat had an idiot and vhass pricing the mustard. And I cried for the idiot vhat vhass life. He vhass life."

"It's terrible," I mumbled, not knowing what to say.

"Don't say this. Vhat is terrible?" she said. "I'm telling you you should know. I'm talking to you.

"That voman, that mother, ve did not say a vord to each other, but ve talked. Not till I came home vhass many hours later did I know ve talked. But ve talked. I heard her and she gave me. Vhat is terrible? You live you talk. Ve talked. And you know vhat I thought vhen I vhass crying?

"I thought: 'I cry tonight now this mother vit her idiot vhat is so beautiful vhat is life tomorrow she vill cry less.' "

SERVING TIME:
THE FIXER

Love is responsibility of an *I* for a *Thou.* In this lies
the likeness of all who love, from the smallest to
the greatest and from the blessedly protected man
to him who is all his life nailed to the cross of the
world, and who ventures to bring himself to the dreadful
point — to love all men.[1]
— Martin Buber

In every generation it is each man's duty to look upon
himself as if he personally had come out of Egypt.
For we are commanded: "Tell your son in that day that
it is because of what the Lord did for *me* when I came
out of Egypt" (Exodus 13:8). It was not only our fore-
fathers whom God saved; He saved us too.[2]
— from the Passover Haggada

The energy of *The Assistant* brings the American — born in
the wilderness — into association with the original exile —
the Jew out of Egypt — and through the union acquaints the
first with the values and direction of the second. The son
returns to the father and the father hands over his
communiqué: *Forward* — the message embedded in a style of
life learned long ago, before he left home. *The Fixer*, the story
of Yakov Bok, goes home, returns to the father, before the
father has any message to give, watches him grow, Morris at
twenty. *The Fixer* educates Bober-Bok so that a generation

later he can educate Frank Alpine — now a young man, once a fatherless boy for whom Bober-Bok first accepted responsibility by signing a note in a prison cell. *The Assistant* deals with the relationship of a man to a man; *The Fixer* deals with the relationship of a man to his history; *The Assistant*, of a son to a father; *The Fixer*, of a son to a fatherland.

The opening scenes in *The Fixer* are of a fatherland in decay. The *shtetl* community — the Jewish purveyor of value and meaning — holds out nothing for Yakov Bok. Drs. Ruth Landes and Mark Zborowski, in their study of the *shtetl*, conclude that "there are three dynamic relationships within the *shtetl* family that constitute an institutional universe and a field of tensions."[3] All three are missing and their lack is referred to again and again in the opening scenes of the book: "These are: the bonds between man and wife, between mother and son, and between father and daughter." It is the absence or presence of Raisl on which each relationship depends, and as such — as I will discuss later — as brief as Raisl's appearance is in the novel, she represents the culmination of what Malamud has been trying to do with his women. Raisl's absence at the book's beginning removes fertility and leaves in its place Dwiora, "a dark uddered cow."[4] Raisl's absence removes family from the *gemeinshaft* and the result is a vacuum: "Opportunity here is born dead" (p.12). But, of course, value *is* here, it is just not visible to the eye of Yakov Bok. To that extent, the sepulchral air of the book's first scenes is as much a matter of a young man's myopia as it is in *The Assistant*: "A death tomb positive." "To discover his own true being," Buber has written, "the Jew must learn to embrace in his mind and heart the entire spirit, or soul, of his people."[5] *The Fixer's* particular *bildungsroman* experience is the growing of Yakov Bok into an awareness of himself through an awareness of his history — the vitality *of* which, and the responsibility *to* which are represented in the energies of the *shtetl* community.

Like Stephen Dedalus, flying by those nets, he must leave his community — his history — in order to understand it. And so he goes off, armed only with a little knowledge — he is, like Alpine, an autodidact — and his phylacteries, forgotten by him and returned by the father-in-law. A little knowledge and the phylacteries, reason and magic — these two pursue Bok throughout his ordeal. Malamud wastes no time endowing the phylacteries with magic powers, [6] as they are passed in their first appearance from father-in-law to son-in-law — only the first of several returns — in a communication as imperfect as the "in-law" is unnatural: "Yakov," says Shmuel, "don't forget your God" (p.20). In truth, the only real link between the two men — Raisl — is there in the phylacteries themselves, as Malamud at once reminds us what is missing in the *shtetl* and gives to the objects the promise of mother: "In the bag was another containing phylacteries. Raisl, before they were married, had made the bag out of a piece of her dress and embroidered it with the tablets of the Ten Commandments" (p.20). Raisl, we will see, rises to the level of Malamud's most fulfilled woman precisely because she and the phylacteries *are* one.

With phylacteries flung in the back of the wagon and a little self-taught philosophy being considered in the front, Yakov Bok — like Spinoza himself — rides away from the Jewish community.

In no time at all he has stripped himself of his former identity. Devoid of beard, he believes correctly that "he doesn't look Jewish" (p.29): The phylacteries are thrown into the river. He finds himself in a church. He abandons his name, his language, his *shtetl*-learned occupation, his dietary laws, the Old Testament, the Kiev ghetto, and — considering his willingness to sleep with the daughter — he abandons his marriage vow (pp. 36, 37, 42, 45, 50, 59). He abandons Raisl, the Seventh Commandment embroidered with the others in her hand. He abandons the phylacteries all over again.

But it is important to note that in giving up one identity he does not assume any new identity. He merely becomes a non-Jew. He does not become a Christian. He has not found any new faith, real or pretended. He is without faith. He runs out of the church ("groped his way on in the dark" [p. 31]). His new name, Yakov Ivanovitch Dologushev, sports un-Christian-like initials. He eats only "those things he had eaten before" (p. 45). He does not consummate a relationship with the daughter or "the ikon of the Holy Mother" (p. 48). He never gets his counterfeit papers. As he told Shmuel upon departing, "A meshummed gives up one God for another. I don't want either" (p. 20).

He is faithless, wandering. When the phylacteries are returned for a second time, in the presence of Passover and the devout old man, Yakov is completely without direction. When the old Jew asks him, "Where is the east?" (p.59), Yakov, disoriented, answers with an impatience that suggests he knows only where the old man's East is. In his study of the phylacteries, Dr. Montague D. Eder finds that "the *tefillin* [phylacteries] ritual is mentioned in connection with the extremely ancient passover festival [where] the father informs his questioning son that the *tefillin* are a sign of memory."[7] But Yakov asks no question, wants no information. He wants only to be free. "So long as a man is set free only in his Self" — this from Buber — " he can do the world neither weal nor woe; he does not concern the world."[8] Yakov's relationship to the world is no relationship, so that, fittingly, having — to his own understanding — freed himself from his Jewishness, he is nonetheless literally imprisoned in the process by a perverse assignation of Jewish identity. "That's what one gets for not knowing which way he's running to begin with," Yakov thinks (p. 85). But after trying to leave first the identity pressed upon him by the *shtetl* and then that pressed upon him by the government, Yakov quits running altogether and begins meeting. He meets his true identity as a Jew.

He arrives at this relationship through the neo-Hasidic mix — a mixing of reason and mystery — of Spinoza and phylacterylike ritual — which has the power to set several perverse situations back on a proper course.

This literary rhythm — a turning through perversity to get us back to a primal, uncorrupted state — is not a new one for Malamud. It appears, though never before so richly, with such success or totality, in all of his previous novels. In *The Natural,* a modern *Faerie Queene*, first Harriet Bird and then Memo Paris is the false Duessa, and the relationships with the baseball player, Roy, are ones of evil, and allurement. Behind Harriet's offered body is a gun and a bullet,[9] and intercourse with Memo, a scene fraught with identity changes, leads astray the New York Knight for most of his quest. At one point in his mistaken journey he and the false damsel, in search of the ocean, end up on the banks of a polluted stream.[10] The suggestion that the knight will be saved from the misdirection this relationship represents comes in the presence of the real princess, Iris Lemon. When Iris desires to see the waters, she takes Roy to a deep and fecund shimmering lake. This signal of a turning through perversity is affirmed at the book's end when Roy acknowledges the fertility of their union.

The same rhythm appears — though with a weakness emblematic of the entire book — in Malamud's *A New Life*. In the near conquering of the waitress Laverne, the romantic Levin sees himself entering into an intimate relationship with nature: "In front of cows, he thought. Now I belong to the ages."[11] In truth, of course, the whole scene is wildly undercut; first, in dialogue — " 'Your breasts smell like hay.' 'I always wash well.' " [12] — and second, in the rather ungracious interruption by the ebullient graduate student. The first union of Levin and Pauline — in the forest — turns through this perversion and leaves us at primacy, origin, innocence: "soft ground among dark conifers . . . the forest gloom broken by rays of sunlight dappling the ground. The wood, pungent with levitating coolness, suggested endless distance and deepest depth . . ." [13] Whether or not we are convinced that this first union blossoms into the kind of love Malamud's story says it does, whether or not the comic and the serious are ever again resolved as nicely as they are here, the fact remains that in this moment we see the rhythm of which we are speaking.

If Malamud uses the dynamics of myth and comedy to establish perversity in the earlier novels, it is sex itself that he turns through in *The Assistant*. Frank Alpine's education — the growing into an awareness of what it is that makes a relationship — is indicated by the change in his dealings with Helen. It is one measure of the great distance the assistant travels when he moves from — in Buber's idiom — the saying of *It* to the saying of *Thou*. When, at the book's end, Frank has, in the most perfect sense, accepted responsibility for Helen, he stands at the end of a journey that began with him climbing a dumbwaiter to spy on her naked body, a voyeur who was — in the words of the author and the spirit of Buber — "making her into a thing" (p. 62).

It is the preponderance of this sort of *I-It* relationship — a twisted, unhappy relationship — that characterizes most of *The Fixer*. The action of the book is moving through this perversity to return Yakov Bok to original value.

These twisted situations include: 1) the corruption of the Passover sacrament, 2) the relationship of the government to Yakov Bok, 3) the relationship of Nicholas II to his people and himself, which acts as a foil for 4) the relationship of Yakov Bok to his people and himself. In each case the two aspects of the enduring dichotomy — reason and ritual, Spinoza and phylacteries, political history and religious history — are perverted.

The story of Passover is the story of sacrifice, faith, holy protection, and initiation. Still unwilling to release the Children of Israel from the House of Bondage after nine searing plagues, the Pharaoh is told by Moses that the firstborn son of every Egyptian will be smitten by the morning. God instructs Moses to have his people sacrifice lambs and smear the blood "upon the doorposts of thy house and upon thy gates," so that the Angel of Death in her journey will *pass over* the houses of the Jews. Moses's people do this. Their children are saved. The Pharaoh, stricken, releases his captives. And the Jews, fearing correctly that the Pharaoh will have a change of heart, make great haste to leave Egypt. The women must seize their dough from the ovens before the yeast has had time to take effect, so that the unleavened bread, or *matzos*, becomes a sign the Jews carry with them into the desert and the beginning of their forty-year pilgrimage to the Promised Land.

In *The Fixer*, Father Anastasy's account of the Jewish sacrament on the occasion of Zhenia Golov's death (which occurs on Passover) totally distorts the Passover story. Having imprisoned Yakov as the ritualistic murderer of the young boy, Father Anastasy has the Jews, not sacrificing lambs, but murdering the firstborn sons themselves; the blood they use not to communicate with their God but for the baking of the *matzos*. (Those who hate Israel," a Hasidic folktale goes, "accuse us of baking the unleavened bread with the blood of Christians. But no, we bake them with the blood of Jews."[14]) The Passover story has the qualities of the vernal myth — sacrificial death, salvation, and regeneration — but Father Anastasy corrupts this spirit by perverting the spirit of the New Testament counterpart, the New Testament's vernal myth, calling the ritual murder "a token of the Jews' eternal enmity against Christendom. . . . They repeat the martyrdom of Christ" (p.110).

A jarring example of the vernal spirit perverted, of initiation perverted, is the incongruity of Yakov's sensations at this time —

In the time the fixer had been in prison the city had turned green and there were sweet-smelling lilacs everywhere but who could enjoy them? Through the open window he could smell the wet grass and new leaves, and where the cemetery ended there were birches with silver trunks. Somewhere nearby an organ grinder was playing a waltz that Zinaida Nikolazvna had played for him once on her guitar, "Summer Is Gone Forever" (p.101).

—all of which take place while the man himself is locked in chains.

But as much as the mythical, mystical quality of Passover is perverted, so too is the other half of the dichotomy I have mentioned — Spinoza-like rationalism — also perverted. After listing the full file of the "desecrations and unspeakable horrors" to which "their Semitic blood directs them," Father Anastasy intones, "in his nasally musical voice," that "perhaps in this age of science we can no longer accept every statement of accusation made against this unfortunate people; however we must ask ourselves how much truth remains despite our reluctance to believe" (p.111).

When this distortion of ritual and reason takes place within the fabric of a relationship it leads to what Buber means by the saying of *It*. We see it in *The Fixer* in the relationships of the government to Yakov, Nicholas II to himself and his people, and Yakov to himself and his people.

The Czarist government wants Yakov to be Jewish, and they want him to be Jewish according to their definition. When he tries to squirm from that definition — when he says he is merely a Jew "by birth and nationality" (p. 75) — the Imperial Government answers, "Let's not complicate matters unnecessarily. Legally you are a Jew." With this Yakov cannot agree. Though he accedes to their demands he does not believe that he is who they say he is: "It's mistaken identity with me" (p. 90).

The identity the government gives Yakov twists the spirit of ritual and reason. Obsessed by what powers they think he has — obsessed by Jewish magic — they search Yakov's body twice daily, head to toe, looking, looking for Jewishness, looking for a thing. The Rationalist spirit Spinoza represents is likewise perverted. "A Jew is a Jew," Grubeshov says. "And that's all there is to it":

> Their history and character are unchangeable. Their nature is constant. This has been proved in scientific studies by Gobineau, Chamberlain and others. We here in Russia are presently preparing one of Jewish facial characteristics." . . . He flipped open a notebook to a page of pen-and-ink sketches, turning the book so that Yakov could read the printing at the top of the page: "Jewish noses" (p.118).

The searching is a bizarre corruption of the intensity of communication on the *I-Thou* level; the scientific quackery refines out of existence the last shred of human feeling. The Imperial Government makes a man into a thing — the ultimate perversion. They know what they want their thing to look like so they let its hair grow long, give it a prayer shawl, *tefillin,* and the other accouterments of the thing they understand to be Jewishness.

But *The Fixer* is the story of Yakov Bok. Yakov is involved in perverse relationships not merely as an innocent victim. Yakov is involved in perversity because there is something gone wrong in him as well. Malamud brings this out beautifully by having him corrupt the spirit of the *mitzvahs.*

The *mitzvah* is that part of Jewish observance that most perfectly blends theology with history. As Doppell and Polish write, "In the texture of Jewish life and thought, a *mitzvah* is a spiritual entity in itself which immortalizes primarily an historic relationship to God which the Jewish people experienced in the course of its history. . . . It flows from an historically spiritual moment when our people confronted God; and every time we enact the *mitzvah* we are re-enacting that spiritual moment of our history in our own times and are renewing it in our own lives as Jews."[15]

The enacting of a *mitzvah* may take its expression in many ways and the word itself is popularly translated "good deed." By the doing of certain good deeds the Jew "relives those historical and spiritual moments of commitment to God . . . moments when he entered into a covenant relationship with God."[16] "He who performs a *mitzvah*," Buber says, "works on the hallowing of the world."[17]

Yakov Bok, at the climax of his education, performs a perfect *mitzvah*. But Malamud has him — lost and godless at the outset — perform two perverse *mitzvahs* first, which represent to us the distance he has to travel.

When Yakov first arrives in Kiev he is without the phylacteries, his beard, his language, his God. He has stripped himself of his Jewish identity. For this reason it is fitting that in helping the drunken Russian — that in performing what appears on the surface to be a *mitzvah* — what results, rather than a covenant relationship, is a business alliance; rather than an encounter with God, he meets an anti-Semite. Rather than a union with the historic, the *mitzvah* results in a denial of the Old Testament; rather than a union with the spiritual, the *mitzvah* results in a near coupling with an "unclean woman."

In later saving an old Jew from a stoning, Yakov again appears to perform a *mitzvah*; but instead, by bringing the abandoned phylacteries into his home, he shows how incapable he is of real *mitzvah*. "*Mitzvos*" — as Doppell and Polish write — "are rooted in the Biblical directive: 'It is a sign between me and the children of Israel forever.' " *Mitzvah* is rooted in the spirit of the phylacteries — the physical symbol of that sign. Those sections of the Bible contained in the phylactery boxes pertain in part to the Passover story, so that the ritual of "tieing on" — the essential *mitzvah* — could be no more timely than during the Passover holiday. "Or take the *mitzvah* of eating *matzos* on *Pesach* [Passover]. It milestones the thrilling encounter of our people with the God of freedom at that turning point in our history when we broke the shackles of Egyptian bondage."[18] But Yakov has forgotten phylacteries, Passover, *matzo*, and *mitzvah*. He has forgotten the spiritual and the historic. He is still in bondage.

As a meeting of history and mystery the *mitzvah* perverted is a perfect symbol of what is wrong with Yakov Bok. Malamud's next step is to drop the symbolic veil and deal with the *mitzvah*'s components directly.

Yakov's problem is that he cannot settle his relationship to the world. He does not know how to relate to history, to two histories, really, to the history of the individual's dealing with individuals, and to the history of the individual's dealing with God.

Yakov, physically cut off from the world, represents, in Buber's terms, the *I* that, alienated from the world, is empty. At the close of one section in *I and Thou*, Buber tells a story about the empty *I*. It seems to speak so primarily to Yakov's situation that I want, for a moment, to try to stand aside and let them converse more directly.

Yakov nearly went mad trying to figure out what was happening to him. What was a poor harmless fixer doing in prison? What had he done to deserve this terrible incarceration, no end in sight? Hadn't he had more than his share of misery in a less than just world? (p. 127).

At times the man, shuddering at the alienation between the I and the world, comes to reflect that something is to be done. As when in the grave night hour you lie, racked by waking dream—bulwarks have fallen away and the abyss is screaming—and note amid your torment: there is still life, if only I got through to it—but how? how?; so is this man in the hours of reflection, shuddering, and aimlessly considering this and that. And perhaps, away in the unloved knowledge of the depths within him, he really knows the direction of turning, leading through sacrifice.[19]

Though he ran in every direction he could not extricate himself from its sticky coils. Who was the spider if it remained invisible? He sometimes thought God was punishing him for his unbelief. He was after all the jealous God. "Thou shalt worship no other Gods before me," not even no Gods.

But he spurned this knowledge; "mysticism" cannot resist the sun of electric light. [20]

Things go badly at a historical moment and go that way, God or no God, forever (p. 127).

He calls thought, in which he rightly has great confidence, to his aid, it shall make good everything for him again. [21]

He tried desperately to put together a comprehensible sequence of events that had led inevitably from his departure from the shtetl to a prison cell in Kiev (p. 127).

And thought paints with its well known speed one—no, two rows of pictures, on the right wall and on the left. On the one there is the universe. The tiny earth plunges from the whirling stars, tiny man from the teeming earth, and now history bears him further through the ages, to rebuild persistently the ant-hill of the cultures which history crushes underfoot. Beneath the row of pictures is written: "One and all." . . . Here he sees that the I is embedded in the world and that there is really no I at all—so the world can do nothing to the I . . . the stream of the world flows over it.[22]

I am in history yet not in it. In a way of speaking I'm far out, it passes me by (p. 55).

On the other wall there takes place the soul. A spinner is spinning the orbits of all stars and the life of all creation and the history of the universe; everything is woven on one thread, and is no longer called stars and creation and universe, but sensations and imaginings, or even experiences, and conditions of the soul. And beneath the row of pictures is written: "One and all." . . . Here he sees that the world is embedded in the I, and that there is really no world at all—so the world can do nothing to the I.[23]

If there was a god after reading Spinoza he had closed up his shop and become an idea. [And Yakov, perverting the Spinozan God, becomes, in a selfish way, a god who becomes an idea.] "It's hard to imitate a dog [d-o-g]. That's not exactly what I mean, but turned around [g-o-d] it is." "You're a martyr for us all" [says the fat Jew before he turns Yakov in (p. 55).]

Another time, if the man shudders at alienation, and the I strikes terror in his heart, he looks up and sees a picture; which picture he sees does not matter, the empty I is stuffed full with the world or the stream of the world flows over it.[24]

It is this disconnectedness—between the *I* and the world, between history and mystery—that makes Yakov empty. If he deals with history he deals with it in a way that denies the self—the self gets swept into the force of history; if he deals with the self or with the spiritual he makes the self into a kind of god and denies the world—the world gets swept into the force of self. On the one hand he makes of the world, of history, a thing; and on the other, he makes of himself—and, significantly, of God—a thing. Between the one thing and the other thing there is no relationship: "Things go badly at an historical moment and go that way, God or no God forever" (p. 127). "Either God is our invention and can't do anything about it, or he's a force in Nature but not in history. A force is not a father" (p. 211).

The growing of Yakov—the making of father—is the coming together of the *I* and the world, of the spiritual and the historic. The union has many names, but one name upon which Malamud, Buber, and Spinoza all agree is "freedom." "The world and I are mutually included, the one in the other," says Buber. "This contradiction in thought, inherent in the situation of *It*, is resolved in the situation of *Thou*, which sets men free from the world in order to bind men up in solidarity of connection with it."[25] This is the freedom about which Yakov nebulously comprehends Spinoza to be talking when the fixer tries to impart his understanding of the philosopher to Bibikov: "Maybe it's that God and Nature are one and the same, and so is man, or some such thing, whether he's rich or poor. If you understand that a man's mind is part of God, then you understand it as well as I. In that way you're free, if you're in the mind of God" (p. 67).

It is when Yakov himself makes this kind of connection — when *I* meets world, when God meets Nature *in man*—that he is freed, literally and spiritually. I return to Buber's story about the man and the pictures—where one picture showed the *I* embedded in the world, and the other showed the world embedded in the *I*: "A moment comes," he says, "when the shuddering man looks up and sees both pictures in a flash together. And a deeper shudder seizes him."[26]

But *things* must get even worse before they get better, before that moment comes. It is spring again—the season of Passover and Easter—and Malamud uses the two stories, as he did with Father Anastasy, to pervert the relationships to history and religion. When Yakov smashes the phylacteries—returned in their magical way for a third time—he makes of history as much an *It* as one could imagine. When "the fixer holds the

broken phylactery to his nose and greedily sucks in the smell"
(p. 189), he reminds us of the prison guards searching inside
his naked body for the substance of Jewishness. The *tefillin's*
message of memory again falls on deaf ears as the fixer's
sacrilege takes place at the very time of year that should most
be commemorated. The scene has about it, properly, the
feeling of rape, of ravage. The phylactery boxes, called the
bayith, or "homes," have been invaded and destroyed by a
stranger. The jewels have been stolen. The covenant has been
broken.

When the phylacteries make their exit—still to return once
more in human form—they are replaced by the New
Testament and the story of the Crucifixion. Here Yakov
climaxes the vision he gradually comes to have of himself as a
god. The story of Christ is the story of a man, of a god, who
knew perfectly Buber's deeper shudder. The dual pictures of a
man given to the world and of the feelings of the world given
to the man come together beautifully in the story of Christ.
Yakov, in his disjointed way, takes just one of the pictures —
of the world's sufferings embedded in a single man — and
makes it his own. His sort of identification with Christ eliminates the flow of one picture to another, perverts Christ and the
mystery of religion; for, as the narrator says, "Nobody suffers
for him and he suffers for no one except himself" (p. 197):

> In the end he was deeply moved when he read how they
> spat on him ["a woman in a hat with velvet flowers spat at
> the fixer" (p. 180)], and beat him with sticks ["As he cried
> out Fetukov reached behind him whipping a short heavy
> stick out of his trousers. He struck Yakov a hard blow"
> (p.124)]; and how he hung on the cross at night. Jesus
> cried out help to God but God gave no help ["Who will
> help me?" (p.129)] (p.190).

When he is given the Old Testament in exchange for the
New, he is back to the relationship to history. While it is still to
him little more than a tale, he does, just the same, "know the
sense of the story," and the attraction is a powerful one:

> He read longer and faster gripped by the narrative of
> the joyous and frenzied Hebrews, doing business, fighting
> wars, sinning, and worshipping — whatever they were

doing always engaged in talk with the huffing puffing God who tried to sound, maybe out of envy, like a human being (p. 196).

While at this point he may be, as the narrator says, "without either the intellectual idea of God or the God of the covenant," he does display a recognition that presages his own story. "He has broken the phylacteries," he has broken the covenant. Still he sees that:

> Israel accepts the covenant in order to break it. That's the mysterious purpose: they need the experience. . . . Suffering they say awakes repentance, at least in those who can repent. Thus the people of the covenant wear out their sins against the Lord. He then forgives them and offers a new covenant. Why not? This is his nature, everything must begin again, don't ask him why. . . . The purpose of the covenant, Yakov thinks, is to create human experience (pp. 196 - 197).

The ideas are in order; what is out of order is that Yakov stands apart from them. He relates to nothing. In getting this said explicitly, Malamud weds the announcement to another man. The sentences, while appearing disjoint, are significantly juxtaposed: "Nobody suffers for him and he suffers for no one except himself. The rod of God's anger against the fixer is Nicholas II, the Russian Csar" (p.197).

In Yakov's feverish evocation of the Prioress's Tale, ideas become men. And once again Yakov, unable to relate, and the Russian Czar, appear together:

> One small-faced boy, a consumptive type, ran from him frantically, his eyes rolling in fright.
> "Stop, I love you," the fixer called to him, but the child never looked back.
> "Once is enough, Yakov Bok."
> Nicholas II appeared, in the white uniform of an admiral of the Russian Navy (p. 205).

The two appear together because at this point the two have much in common. Neither can relate to another. Yakov's saying of *Thou* is a bad one. This is almost parodied in

Nicholas's inability to communicate on any level. When Yakov says, "Little Father, you'll never meet a more patriotic Jew. Tears fill my eyes when I see the flag. Also I'm not interested in politics, I want to make a living. Live and let live, if you don't mind my saying so," Nicholas answers. "My dear fellow, don't envy me my throne."! And yet Yakov himself, who merely listens to stories and holds himself apart from their blood, demonstrates the same kind of detachment as Nicholas, dressed in white, sailing off by himself, into the Black Sea, in his white boat.

But Yakov is not Nicholas. He is able to kill the Nicholas in him. When he talks of suffering he wears the clothes of the sufferer; when Nicholas talks he wears white crisp and white clean. And out of all this suffering Yakov learns about relationship. He comes to understand that others suffer and he reacts to his understanding. In fact, he finds in other people the very reason to go on living. This discovery, this growth, this connection takes place in a brief segment (pp. 219 - 224) that is structurally different from anything in the book. It is written in the present tense. Buber, not unexpectedly, has some interesting things to say about time:

> The *I* of the primary word *I-It*, that is, the *I* faced by no *Thou*, but surrounded by a multitude of "contents," has no present, only the past.
> The present, and by that is meant not the point which indicates from time to time in our thought merely the conclusion of "finished" time, the mere appearance of a termination which is fixed and held, but the real, filled present, exists only in so far as actual presentness, meeting, and relation exist. The present arises only in virtue of the fact that the *Thou* becomes present.[27]

And the *Thou* becomes present when Yakov holds off the approaching hearse, when he finds a reason to continue:

> What do I get by dying, outside of release from pain? What have I earned if a single Jew dies because I did? Suffering I can gladly do without, I hate the taste of it, but if I must suffer let it be for something . . . he is afraid to die

. . . because there is no way of keeping the consequences of his death to himself. . . . If the fixer stands accused of murdering one of their children, so does the rest of the tribe (p. 222).

Nowhere is *The Fixer's* story more universal, more instructive for all. Yakov Bok decides he must live because if he does not others will die. Yakov Bok decides that if it will save others he will endure the suffering of existence. In the spirit of Buberian paradox, Yakov Bok frees himself from the world by binding himself to it. Yakov Bok makes of his life relation.

Only moments before this decision he had identified with the practiced detachment of the prison guard:

"Don't think I am not aware of your misfortunes, Bok, because I am. It's a terrible thing to see a man in chains . . . but to be frank with you I try not to dwell on it much. The nerves can take just so much, and I already have all the worry I can stand. I think you know what I mean by that."
Yakov says he does (p. 221).

He knows only too well — but never again so well; for moments after the decision he makes a covenant with the Children of Israel by making a covenant with himself:

He pities their fate in history. . . . So what can Yakov Bok do about it? All he can do is not make things worse. He's half a Jew himself, yet enough of one to protect them. After all, he knows the people; and he believes in their right to be Jews and live in the world like men. He is against those who are against them. He will protect them to the extent that he can. This is his covenant with himself. If God's not a man he has to be (p. 223).

No Jew in the beginning, half a Jew now, Yakov needs only to effect his promise, to be wholly Jewish, and, that way, a person. The opportunity arrives in the form of Malamud's most perfectly conceived woman — Raisl Bok.

Though her arrival at the prison is her first fleshly appearance, Raisl's spirit has been present throughout the book. She is wife and mother, the phylacteries, Israel, the promise of community and salvation. She is Iris Lemon *and* Memo Paris; she is Pauline Gilley *and* Avis Fliss. She is more than Helen Bober.

Malamud's women have all been representative of the great stories from which they came. They, like their stories, offer the promise of salvation. The woman as sexual partner, as the bearer of new life, as menstruating, swelling, deflating, seasonable creature, has been an important partner to Malamud's suffering protagonists. But there have been none so caught up in the weave of the tale, none so whole as Raisl Bok.

Serving in the limited capacity that befits the fair damsel, Iris Lemon, in *The Natural,* comes out of nowhere, is developed quickly in a few extensive passages, and is just enough of a person to stand up at the story's end as Roy Hobbes's hope for a better life. Her character is spotless — her misfortune coming through no lack of her own — so that, true to the spirit of allegory, she needs to be combined with at least one other character to even approach the shape of a whole human being. Memo Paris, with her ailing breasts, bringing disease into the kingdom, does what is two-dimensionally asked of her. The women of *The Natural* are not in themselves human creatures. Human creatures combine in order and disorder within a single frame.

But *The Natural* never purports to have a cast of human creatures. *A New Life* does. Pauline Gilley, whose meager breasts, at the story's end, swell with the flow of a mother's milk, just cannot hold up on her thin, white shoulders all the sorts of salvation she is supposed to represent. She is asked to save Sy Levin — from himself, from his romanticism, from the comic frame of the novel; she is asked to save herself — but from what? Do we really know her? She is asked to save the book and she just can't do it. Malamud needs a love that cannot be grown in the world he has created. The relationship between Pauline and Seymour seems as insubstantial, as pathetically desperate, and as selfish, as that between Seymour and Avis, lumpy of breast and only half conceived. *A New Life* is an interesting failure. It is intriguing that the novel's one consistent symbol, the photograph — Levin's application shot, Gilley's picture of his wife on the beach, the picture

Gilley takes of the departing couple on their way to a new life — brings us to the novel's ultimate problem — the resolution of identity. Pauline Gilley, the novel's heroine, is no more nor less interesting a failure.

In *The Assistant*, Helen Bober is beautifully drawn, in a tightly controlled story about relationship. She is the consummation of Frank's education, the promise of new life, regeneration, and effected salvation. Her hopes, her seriousness, her perception, and her beauty are special weights that hang from different corners of the novel's universe, compressing it, closing it in upon its inhabitants. But the escape, the freedom, the decompression are really the events of the novel's afterlife. *The Assistant* is not the story of Frank and Helen's relationship, and as finely wrought as she is, it is no criticism of Malamud to say that she is not as thoroughgoing a character as Raisl Bok.

From the beginning Raisl has been the community. The book opens upon the *shtetl* in decay, upon value in decay, and Raisl, having run off with another man, having broken the marriage vow, is herself in decay. She too has forgotten the covenant. Having once given a part of herself to the phylacteries, literally and figuratively, she has cast off memory in the way of her husband. Still, that part of her that first went into the phylacteries follows Yakov throughout the novel, rises up out of the river, and returns, so that the phylacteries, the covenant, Raisl herself are the promise of regeneration and return. "God forgives them," as Yakov has said, "and offers a new covenant. . . . This is his nature, everything must begin again, don't ask him why."

Barren throughout her marriage, Raisl presents Yakov with a son; though not his naturally, she gives him the opportunity — if he will forgive, if he will assume responsibility, if he will help — to claim a son as his own. Raisl's fertility implies his sterility. His role in the downfall of the marriage — of several marriages — is manifest. Psychoanalytically oriented students of the phylactery ritual repeatedly point out its phallic quality. ("In fact the Eastern Jews call the scrotum in vulgar parlance, the *tefillin* bag."[28]) In offering him a son, Raisl offers Yakov his sexual equipment, the *tefillin*, the covenant, his heritage. It was the absence of these things, all bound up within the character of wife, that made him infertile. Raisl offers Yakov the opportunity to be, literally, the man of *aboda*: the man who "collects himself." She asks Yakov to accept her, that is, to accept Israel, the repentant harlot of Hosea's harangue. She asks, "Forgive me. Forgive the past" (p. 233). She says, in effect, "I am Israel. Accept me and accept the father. Accept me and be made a father." "Take heed to thy self, and keep thy soul diligently," it says in the phylactery scrolls, "lest thou forget the things which thine eyes saw, and lest they depart from thy heart all the days of thy life; but make them known unto thy children and thy children's children" (Deuteronomy 4:9).

And Yakov accepts. Reason and mystery come together. In his attraction for her he listens to his mind ("What's there to do here but think, so I've thought") and to his blood ("He felt as he watched her the weight of the blood in his heart" [p. 234]). He is led to call her son his own: *B'nai B'rith*, the Children of Israel, the Children of the Covenant. He effects the covenant made earlier to himself, rejoins in spirit the community of the *shtetl*, performs a perfect *mitzvah*. He becomes one, the man of *aboda*. History and the *I* come together:

> It snows history, which means what happens to somebody starts in a web of events outside the personal. It starts of course before he gets there. We're all in history, that's sure, but some are more than others, Jews more than some. He had to his painful surprise stepped into history more deeply than others (p. 225).

He joins the world. "He was the experience. . . . He was somebody else than he had been" (p. 256). Knowing it or not, history and religion come together: "It was history that counted — the world's bad memory. It remembered the wrong things. So for a Jew it was the same wherever he went, he carried a remembered pack on his back" (p. 255). This is the sort of history Buber has in mind when he says, "Religion is history." "The Jews," he has said, "are a community based on memory. A common memory has kept us together and enabled us to survive." [29]

Yakov has had a meeting. He needs only to do as Raisl asks — to come home. But Canaan is not entered in the life of the novel. The last passage in the phylactery scrolls shows the Jews only just about to leave the desert. Still, a union, in a world without unions, has been made. The seeds of salvation have been sown. The promise of a return to health is in the air. When it is demanded that Yakov, dressed and ready for his trial, be searched a final time, the prison guard, Kogin, who had spoken earlier about the necessity of detachment, is won over to the world of relationship. The action of a minor character, so long a part of the diseased universe, being saved in the final moments of his life as he strikes a blow and is himself stricken, is a perfect replica of the close of *King Lear's* third act. Here the First Servant is unable to stand by as Gloucester's eyes are blinded:

Hold your hand, my lord.
I have served you ever since a child,
But better service have I never done you
Than now to bid you hold (III.vii.71-74).

The effects of the two scenes are identical. They make us aware of the poverty of such unions heretofore, and indicate that the forces of order are marshaling troops in the wings waiting to storm the stage.

Yakov storms the stage, demonstrates the distance he has come, when he murders Nicholas II, and the empty *I*. Malamud, a modern master of magic, uses this brief fantasy to point up the real character of the fixer's enemy — that enemy which lurked within and without — and by having the enemy expunged declares an end to perversity and a return to the proper course.

The emptiness of Nicholas's relationship to his people, his country, his heritage is clearly brought out in Buber's dialogue about Napoleon:

— But how if a man's mission require him to know nothing but connexion with his particular Cause, that is, no longer to know any real relation with or present realisation of a *Thou* — to have everything about him become an *It*, serving his particular Cause? What of Napoleon's saying of the *I*? Is it not legitimate? Is this phenomenon of experiencing and using not a person?

— He had no one whom he recognised as a being. He was for millions the demonic *Thou*, the *Thou* that does not respond, that responds to *Thou* with *It*, that does not respond genuinely in the personal sphere but responds only in his own sphere, his particular Cause, with his own deeds. This demonic *Thou*, to which no one can become *Thou*, is the elementary barrier of history, where the basic word of connexion loses its reality, its character of mutual action. Towering in times of destiny, fraught with destiny, towards him everything flames, but his fire is cold. To him a thousand several relations lead, but from him none. [30]

And Yakov, once as spiritually destitute, once so very like this man in all but the grandeur of his role, is now nothing like him. Where he was once a Little Father to whom a whole history said *Thou* and he heard nothing, he is now a real father who hears *Thou* and answers *Thou* in return:

"Permit me to ask, Yakov Shepsovitch, are you a father?"
"With all my heart."

For *Yakov*, as for Stephen Dedalus, the long night ends when the feeling is overcome that history itself "is a nightmare from which I must awake."

The Fixer is the story of a man who, by enduring incredible suffering in the name of an unnamed faith that there is in the world still a place for value, unconsciously denies the absurdity of existence and has awakened within him that human grace which teaches a man that a force *is* a father, connects him to his history, and allows him as he rides into the open world to be identified.

EPILOGUE
The Assistant and *The Fixer:* Novels of Connection

> All real living is meeting.
> — Martin Buber

The Assistant and *The Fixer* share rhythms and textures, character and conscience; they are stories of imprisonment, real and effective, of the man of *aboda, serving time,* who, through suffering and endurance, grows into an idea and stands, at the story's end, on the border of the Promised Land.

The Assistant takes a man out of the world and brings him to an individual. *The Fixer* takes an individual and brings him to the world. The energy is the same. Only the directions are different:

> IDA TO MORRIS: "Why do I cry? I cry for the world.
> I cry for my life that it went away wasted. I cry for you"
> (p. 117).

> YAKOV: "What are you crying for?"
> RAISL: "For you, for me, for the world" (p. 234).

The two directions together give us the pulsating blood of relationship, of connection to the circumambient universe, of *I* and *Thou.* The stuff of transcendence is within this pulse: "When he, even he who abhors the name God and believes himself to be godless, gives his whole being to addressing the *Thou* of his life, as a *Thou* that cannot be limited by another, he addresses God." [31]

The Assistant and *The Fixer* are novels of beginning. They are the stories of new life rising out of the ashes of another man and another world. They are the stories of Passover and of circumcision, historically linked, Roheim tells us: "Passover must once have been a vernal initiation ceremony. In combination with this ceremony we find circumcision, a passage through or into something."[32] They are the stories of a first step into the Promised Land, and of a first step out of the desert. They are the stories of young men entering into manhood. They are stories of the relation of private to public season.

"And in the beginning," says Martin Buber, "is relation."

farbrengen

As I turned to leave I saw him pulling something from his pocket for my inspection. "Take this," he said, handing me a dime. "And give it to a poor man in Boston."

"For you?"

"For you. No harm can come to one who is on his way to perform a mitzvah."

THE ECSTASY
OF AUGIE MARCH

The dance of life, the whole story of our wanderings; in a labyrinth of error, the labyrinth of this world. We wandering in the wilderness: Israel; Aeneas and his band of brothers to find Rome; Brute and his band of brothers to find Britain; the band of pilgrims . . . from England to New England . . . [1]

— Norman O. Brown

The saint is a traveller. . . . Such is the way of ecstasy. [2]

— Martin Buber

Love is an existence which lives in a kingdom larger than the kingdom of individuals. It is in truth the Bond of Creation, that is, it is in God. Life covered and guaranteed by life, life emptying itself into life, not until you realize this can you perceive the soul of the world. [3]

— Martin Buber

Finishing one of his characteristically passion-blown outbursts, Augie March compels his listener to answer, "What you are talking about is *moha* — a Navajo word, and also Sanskrit, meaning the opposition of the finite. It is the Bronx cheer of the conditioning forces. Love, being infinite, is the only answer to *moha*. I mean all the forms of love: eros, agape, libido, philia, and ecstasy. They are always the same but sometimes one quality dominates." [4] Love is the only answer. In Saul Bellow's *The Adventures of Augie March*, ecstasy is the quality that dominates: love, in the form of ecstasy, what the Hasids mean by *hitlahabut*, is the only answer.

Bernard Malamud conveys the spirit of *aboda*, of devotion, of discipline, of serving time. *Aboda* is a preparation for *hitlahabut*, for fervor and release, for "going at things free style," as Augie puts it. "Everybody knows," Augie says with customary caution, "there is no fineness or accuracy of suppression; if you hold down one thing you hold down the adjoining" (p. 5). And so, nothing is held down. *Augie March* is not what they call "a tightly controlled novel." But the question of a novel's form is not, as I have explained, central to the concerns of our work. The several problems inherent in *Augie March* are taken up more fully and more properly in the next chapter — which deals with form within the context of our own goals. It is enough to say now that the novel is perhaps not a perfect expression of *hitlahabut*, since, as Buber says, "Repetition, that power which weakens and enfeebles so much in the life of man, has *no effect* upon Ecstasy, which is rekindled over and over again by the most ordinary and uniform events."[5] If the flame is sometimes a little slow to rekindle, still the novel, all in all, packs as great a charge, stands ready to propel Augie and the reader over as wide a panorama, as any yet seen in the literature of this century. The explosion sends the record crashing in every direction, each direction seeming perhaps no less expendable than the next. The volume of the explosion is tremendous: nearly a quarter of a million words go flying before the author is "done speaking . . . through stirring" (p. 539). And when the quiet comes, when peace stills the Sound and the Fury the author calls up on his very first page (an idiot baby brother babbles by a "curl-wired fence"), something of value is certainly signified. *Hitlahabut*, we will see, is itself a preparation for *shiflut*.

By demanding a specific and consistent contribution from both the *bildungsroman* and the picaresque, Bellow brings the forms together to achieve a new vibration in the novel: the rogue moves, brings place and space to the reader's eye, pushes back the covers and reveals . . . the wasteland, the spiritual rot, the sparks entrapped, the soul, in cellophane, a thing to package and to trade; the young man quests, brings progress and resistance, brings growth, brings time into the novel, and is educated . . . to the mystery, the infinite, to the holy, to humility. That the young man in search of the holy is also a picaro, that the search goes on on the horizon, *in this world* — these conditions actually define the Hasidic stance: "The salvation of man does not lie in his holding himself far removed from the worldly, but in consecrating the worldly to holy, to divine meaning: his work and his food, his rest and his wandering, the structure of the family and the structure of society. It lies in his preserving the great love of God for all creatures, yes, for all things."[6]

Augie's difficulties in preserving the great love of God, in himself, and in his world, make up the one coherent conflict in the book. Whenever roguery and spiritual quest come together tension results: as Augie March is born of a rogue's union with a creature of love, the conflict goes on within him continually; his paternal inheritance, keeping him entangled with the world outside, leads him to continual external conflict as well, since the spiritual poverty he finds there, once entangled, does battle with the progress of his education. While the triumph of the novel is Augie's election and comprehension of the spiritual over the rogue within him, the paternal inheritance proves vital in the process, since if it were not for Augie's "opposition," repeatedly flinging him back into the world, he would never learn that this is precisely where his search is to be concluded. And this is Augie's education: to understand first, his powers as a human being, and, second, that the play and practice of these powers must take place in the daily life. As Augie struggles to this knowledge, Bellow casts in his path a tragicomic grotesquerie: "The Valley of the Bones," staged by Cecil B. De Mille; the mechano-technical world at its worst.

But as an antidote to this overwhelming portrayal of the life of *It*, Bellow, with still greater enthusiasm, brings to life the being Buber calls "the man of grace." Bellow's own praising, his own adoring of Augie's qualities, of Augie's humanness, enriches the religious texture of the novel. Any literary glossary will say of the picaresque novel that it is "held together largely because the episodes happen to one person."[7] But the holy concern of *Augie March* lifts this definition from the level of simple fact to the level of literary insight: the idea that a story can be kept going purely because a person stays alive, because a person lives; the idea that a person *is* plot, *is* story, that humanness, the very fact of being, is novel — this casts a person in the consummate activity: that of carrying on a dialogue with being.

Augie reaches the first stage in his education when he decides in favor of that part of his character given him by his mother — "I was well-stocked, probably by inheritance, in all the materials of love" (p. 51). But before the decision is made, Augie must move through the magnetic fields of those who would pull him in the other direction, of those who would pull him to themselves, to spiritual frustration or decay. Augie must move through the positions of alienation and accommodation — the two great "answers of concession."

The first such field is in Augie's own home. Like the *shtetl* of Yakov Bok, the family, the community is in decay: literally — the father is missing, a stranger rules; and spiritually — there is Grandma Lausch, the first in a long line of Machiavelles, instructing, "Nobody asks you to love the whole world. . . . The more you love people the more they'll mix you up. A child loves, a person respects" (p.11); and there is Georgie, who, when "he began to do with his soul" (p. 62), could only moan and run his feelings back to their source, an idiot condemned to spiritual circularity. Grandma Lausch and Georgie, shaped in the book's first strokes, reveal the extremes of the wasteland — premeditative manipulator and innocent victim. Both have their souls locked away, and both, indeed, are institutionalized before the book ends.

Another dangerous magnetic attraction in Augie's early life is that which surrounds William Einhorn, user extraordinaire; cripple, naturally:

> Like Grandma Lausch again, he knew how to use large institutions . . . it was his special pride that he knew how to use the means contributed by the age to connive as ably as anyone else. . . . Find Einhorn in a serious mood . . . and he'd give you the lowdown on the mechanical age . . . and the kind of advantage that had to be taken of it . . . this was what you heard: . . . whether they screwed or were screwed, whether they themselves did the manipulating or were roughly handled . . . (pp. 75-77).

"The history of the individual and that of the human race," Buber tells us, "indicate a progressive augmentation of the world of *It* . . . the primary connection of man with the world of *It* is comprised in using. . . . The development of the ability to use comes about mostly through the decrease of man's

power to enter into relation — the power in virtue of which alone man can live the life of the spirit. . . . We only need to fill each moment with using and it ceases to burn." [8]
But Augie is a burner, a man of ecstasy. Even in the midst of this use and abuse he demonstrates qualities that would identify him with the *zaddikim*: the priority of the present over the future — "I had a weak sense of consequences" (p. 46); a constitutional inclination to love — "the danger of our blood . . . we were susceptible to love" (p. 145); the quest for fulfillment — "I know I longed very much, but I didn't understand for what" (p. 89); a suspicion of logic and mental persuasion — "Talk will lead people on until they convince their minds of things they can't feel true" (p. 218).

Augie feels things true. More compelling even than his characteristic "position statements" are the easy, ambling, word-shaped settings he takes time from his pilgrimage to describe. In this kind of telling, in this kind of spontaneous involvement with the object he wants us to view, Augie shows himself unable to objectify, shows himself to be a man of relation rather than experience. In this way we become aware from the outset that in Augie we are in the presence of a man with power — a power that proves the power of the mechanical age to be puny beside it — the power of *Thou*, the power to feel — however *in potentia* the power may be — that "God can be beheld," as Buber says, "in every object and in each pure deed":

> I sometimes went alone; she didn't see why I should want to. Nor did she see what I strayed into town for in the morning, or why I took pleasure in sitting in the still green bake of the Civil War courthouse square after my thick breakfast of griddle cakes and eggs and coffee. But I did, and warmed my belly and shins while the little locust trolley clinked and crept to the harbor and over the trestles of the bog-spanning bridge where the green beasts and bulrush-rocking birds kept up their hot, small-time uproar. I brought along a book, but there was too much brown stain on the pages from the sun. The benches were white iron, roomy enough for three or four old gaffers to snooze on in the swamp-tasting sweet warmth that made the redwing blackbirds fierce and quick and the flowers frill, but other living things slow and lazy-

blooded. I soaked in the heavy nourishing air of this be-
friending atmosphere like rich life-cake, the kind that
encourages love and brings on a mild pain of emotions. A
state that lets you rest in your own specific gravity, and
where you are not a subject matter but sit in your own
nature, tasting original tastes as good as the first man . . .
(p. 142).

Augie displays from the beginning the essence of the
Hasidic spirit: "original tastes as good as the first man": the
key to this spirit, Buber says, "is the 'ever anew' of each
situation as opposed to the 'once-for-all' with which man tries
to abstract himself from the concrete";[9] "Creation does not
merely take place once in the beginning but also at every
moment throughout the whole of time."[10] The person of this
spirit is the person of ecstasy, and it is ecstasy that Augie's
fellows see in his face when they say to him, "Same healthy
color as always, and smiling away" (p. 54); or "You'll die like
everybody else. But I have to admit, that's not what you make
people think of when they look at you. You're a pretty gay
numero" (pp. 206 - 207).

Thus the question at the book's beginning is not whether
Augie has the potential to be a man of grace, but whether he
will grow, whether he will choose or be able to honor — to
hallow — his own gift, or whether he will be swayed or suf-
focated by the magnetic fields of manipulation and desecration. His gift pulls him in one direction, but those who have
already neglected their own pull him in another. All around
him, the voices of compromising accommodation: "Take it!
Take, take if they give you. Never refuse" (p. 193); "Renling
and I will be your parents because we will give you, and all the
rest is bunk" (p. 160); "Cold-blooded! What's cold-blooded
about it? . . . Why be fooling around to make this perfect
great marriage? What's it going to save you from?" (p. 208);
"Nobody's ever been laid better at any price" (p. 226). It is the
tension between Augie's gift and this graveyard that results in
what Einhorn correctly labels Augie's "opposition — "You've
got opposition in you" (p. 123). "The coincidentia oppositor-
um." Buber calls it, "the coincidence of oppositions of feelings."[11] It is this opposition that makes Augie the Jewish
picaro, a picaro with a problem; a happy wanderer, but heavy;
aimless, yet in search.

But Augie does grow. He takes the first step. He chooses to honor his gifts; to have mercy, as the Hasids say, on the holy sparks; to help them escape. He has a special moment with a set of books and is awakened, first, to his own powers: "I had found something out about an unknown privation, and I realized how a general love or craving, before it is explicit or before it sees its object, manifests itself as boredom or some other kind of suffering. And what did I think of myself in relation to the great occasions, the more sizable being of these books. Why, I *saw* them, first of all . . . I could *see*, so there nevertheless was a share for me in all that had happened" (p. 203). In touch now with being, knowing more of his privation, Augie throws himself into a quest to find a life of perpetual pure moments. But in this first declaration he reveals how very far along he has to go:

> "Well, now, who can really expect the daily facts to go, toil or prisons to go, oatmeal and laundry tickets and all the rest, and insist that all moments be raised to the greatest importance, demand that everyone breathe the pointy, star-furnished air at its highest difficulty, abolish all brick, vaultlike rooms, all dreariness and live like prophets or gods? Why everybody knows this triumphant life can only be periodic. So there's a schism about it, some saying only this triumphant life is real and others that only the daily facts are. For me there was no debate, and I made speed into the former (p. 204).

Augie's education from this point on, of course, consists in his learning that in fact there is not "a schism about it," that "this triumphant life" and "the daily facts" are one. "At each place, in each hour, in each act, in each speech, the holy can blossom forth."[12] Augie's understanding of a separation is a perfect example of Buber's *I-It* dynamic: "Taking his stand in the shelter of the primary word of separation, which holds off the *I* and the *It* from one another, he has divided his life with his fellow men into two tidily circled-off provinces, one of institutions and the other of feelings — the province of *It* and the province of *I*. Institutions are 'outside,' where all sorts of aims are pursued, where a man works, negotiates, bears influence, undertakes, concurs. . . . Feelings are 'within,' where life is lived."[13]

Still, Augie, in trying to leave the world of *It* entirely, has made a first step. He is looking for the triumphant life. He understands his energy as a "restlessness to be taken up into something greater than myself" (p. 213). His brother decides his problem is that "you're looking for the best there is" (p. 208). And from here on, Augie comes increasingly closer to finding it. His is an education to ecstasy. His wandering does not lack a goal, only a finality. He is on the threshold of living the life the Hasidim call the life of "Holy Insecurity": " 'Holy Insecurity' is life lived in the Face of God. It is the very opposite of any security of salvation. . . . The meeting with God takes place in the 'lived concrete,' and lived concreteness exists only insofar as the moment retains its true dialogical character of presentness and uniqueness."[14]

And from here on Bellow's depictions of desecration are more striking for Augie's aversion to and effect upon them. In the presence of the Magnus family, Augie cogently conveys the philosophy of mechano-technical royalty, expounding the dynamics of *It* as well as Buber himself: "In this modern power of luxury with its battalions of service workers and engineers, it's the things themselves, the products that are distinguished, and the individual man isn't nearly equal to their great sum. Finally they are what becomes great — the multitude of baths with never-failing hot water, the enormous air-conditioning units and the elaborate machinery. No opposing greatness is allowed, and the disturbing person is the one who won't serve by using" (p. 250).

And Augie will not serve by using. The Magnus Life — the Great Life, as it is seen by many — is one "in which I didn't fundamentally believe" (p. 251). And in what does he fundamentally believe? On marrying Lucy Magnus, he says, "I could have done so from love, but not to get to the objective" (p. 261).

Augie March, the man of love, the man who carries the Hasid's banner: "One of the fundamental sentences of the Hasids," Buber says, "is to love more."[15] When Mimi Vellers — the most wonderful female of Bellow's creation — says to Augie, "You take my side, don't you? You can see the point of love, I mean" (p. 278), Augie tells us, "I saw no necessity to answer." Augie learns a great deal from Mimi and from his own response to her. Bellow, himself, is so in love with this girl that his own hallowing makes a rare personal appearance, as he fixes in our memory one of the book's most moving pictures, not in the exuberant overwriting voice of his persona, but in a simple and direct private statement that celebrates the vitality of the human spirit: Having just aborted her pregnancy at the hands of a near-butcher, blood-drained and heartsick, Mimi is helped down the stairs by her friend Augie. Arms clasped around him, leaning on his back for support, Bellow tells us, "When her head rolled on my shoulder and approached my neck, she drew on the skin of it with her lips" (p. 283). Augie takes away a lesson from this display: "She was confirming that no matter what complication, injury, foulness, she didn't back down from her belief that all rested on the gentleness in privacy of man and woman" (p. 284). (The holiness of scenes like this, and Bellow's subsequent support of the lesson Augie learns, should be themselves enough to show how wrong Marcus Klein is when he uses the word "accommodation" to describe his sense of an end to alienation in Bellow's fiction.[16])

Augie learns. He grows. He moves decidedly closer to dissolving that schism between "the daily facts" and "the triumphant life": "I had the idea that . . . if the highest should come in that empty overheated tavern with its flies and the hot radio buzzing between the plays and plugged beer from Sox Park, what are you supposed to do but take the mixture and say imperfection is always the condition as found; all great beauty too, my scratched eye-balls will always see scratched. And there may gods turn up anywhere" (p. 273). The distinction remains, but the two — however grudgingly — have come together. (This is a kind of accommodation. If Augie's education ended here, Klein's argument would have greater weight.)

Augie March, the man of love, of Holy Insecurity, assured of nothing, unknowing of what it is he seeks, knowing only that he needs, continues his quest. Having gotten a little closer, his effect upon, and his response to, the world of *It* is even more dramatic. His reunion with Jimmy Klein, for example, is precipitated by an apparently unfortuitous turn of events: Augie is a captured book thief; Jimmy is the observant store detective. When they meet for coffee to discuss the situation it appears that Augie is wallowing in what the Hasid would call "a lower rung" — he is a common thief, not even a very good one, badly in need of money; and it appears that Jimmy has transcended his former indiscretions — he is now a man of authority, respectable, responsibly connected with a large corporation. Yet when the interview is over, it is clear that Jimmy, stripped by circumstance and weakness of even the slightest shred of spirituality ("Don't you know how it is by now? It's all that you want from life comes to you as one single thing — fucking" [p. 281]), is the impoverished one, and that Augie, stealing purely out of feeling for his distressed friend ("I let him think that I was Mimi's lover, for otherwise it would have been difficult to make him understand" [p. 282]), is a very wealthy man. Augie March, the man of ecstasy: "Same jerk as you always were. A train could hit you and you'd think it was just swell and get up with smiles, like knee-deep in June" (p. 279).

But most striking of all, perhaps, at this place in Augie's pilgrimage, are Kayo Obermark's words on Man, which at once continue, with new emphasis, Bellow's panorama of the wasteland's populace and at the same time, by their direct opposition to Hasidic thought and Augie March, point up the man of grace he is becoming: "Kayo thought the greatest purity was outside human relations, that those only begot lies and cabbage-familiarity, and he told me, 'I prefer stones any time. I could be a geologist. I'm not even disappointed in humankind, I just don't care about it, and if there's one thing that's sure, it's that this world is certainly not enough, and if there isn't any more they can have it all back' " (p. 272).

This world is enough for Augie March. In fact, it is becoming, as he is becoming, more and more in each episode. He continues his affair with the universe, relating to his surroundings as an *I* to a *Thou*: "I was stirred in all kinds of ways, including the soft shuffle in the tree-top of leaves just broken out of the thick red barks. . . . And this lightness of mind — I could have benefited from the wisdom about it that the heavy is the root of the light. First, that is, that the graceful comes out of what is buried at great depth. But wisdom has to spread and knot out in all directions" (p. 316).

Wisdom spreads and knots out; and the digging continues. In the midst of his affair with Thea, Augie puts into words his sense of the nature of his quest: "I had looked all my life for the right thing to do, for a fate good enough. I had opposed people in what they wanted to make of me, but now that I was in love with her I understood much better what I myself wanted" (p. 333).

And what he wanted was to perpetuate the feeling he had for and around Thea — the feeling of an *I* for a *Thou*: "It seemed as if an exchange or transfer had happened of us both into still another person who hadn't existed before. There was a powerful feeling of love" (p. 325). And the feeling of love, Bellow does not miss the opportunity to say, is a holy feeling: "If I had been on my bent knees . . . praying . . . I think it would have been no different" (p. 325). "Every particular *Thou*," writes Buber, "is a glimpse through to the eternal *Thou*." [17]

Direction is the difference between Buber and Bellow: the theologian begins by stating his case and moves to metaphor for clarity; the novelist begins with the metaphor and, in the end, has given it life enough to state the case for itself. Thus of Augie March, the man of ecstasy: "When a man ardently desires a woman." Buber writes, explaining the dynamics of *hitlahabut*, "he sees her many-colored garments, but his mind does not dwell on their ornamentation and color, but on the glory of her whom he desires, and whom the garments enfold. Others see the garments and no more. So he, who in truth desires and embraces God, in all things of the world sees only the power and pride of the Creator who Himself dwells in all things." [18] "Any no-account thing," says Augie, "such as her walking to the kitchen or bending to pick up an object from the floor, when I would see the shape of her back, her spine, or the soft departure of her breasts, or her brush, made my soul topple over. I loved her to the degree that anything she chanced to do was welcome to me" (p. 326). "I was threaded to her as if through the skin. Any trifling object she took pleasure in could become important to me at once; anything at all, a comb or hairpin or a piece of line, a compass inside a tin ring . . ." (p. 330). "Every particular *Thou* is a glimpse through to the eternal *Thou*." The man of ecstasy sees the Loved One in all things of the world. "But he who has not reached this stage sees things and God as though they were separate." [19]

Augie's education is advancing. He reaches this stage; he falls back from it; he reaches it again. He has his moments. In his ecstasy with Thea, "the triumphant" and "the daily facts" — the words he himself gave to the separation — have come together for the first time without qualification or a mood of concession to life's imperfection. In each successive advance to the stage the dialogue with the holy is more sustained, more accomplished, more ecstatic. "In ecstasy," Buber tells us, "all the past and the future turn into the present. Time crumbles, the limits of Eternity vanish; only the moment remains and the moment is Eternity."[20] Augie March has his moments: "Some things I have an ability to see without feeling much previous history, almost like birds or dogs that have no human condition but are always living in the same age, the same at Charlemagne's feet as on a Missouri scow or in a Chicago junkyard" (p. 342). As Buber says, "The central reality of the everyday hour on earth . . . a streak of sun on a maple twig" — this gives the man of ecstasy "a glimpse of the eternal *Thou*."[21] Says Augie March: "I fix my memory down to an ant in the folds of bark or fat in a piece of meat or colored thread on the collar of a blouse. Or such discrimination as where on a bush of roses you see variations in heats" (p.342). "In the beginning is relation," writes Martin Buber, retelling Genesis. "Spirit in its human manifestation is a response of man to his *Thou* . . . the response to the *Thou* which appears and addresses him out of the mystery. Only in virtue of his power to enter into relation is he able to live in the spirit."[22] And here it is, the dialogue: the man of ecstasy hears his *Thou* and responds. And Augie March is close, he tries: he says of the things he sees in his universe that they "make your breast and bowel draw at various places from your trying to correspond . . . make you attempt to answer and want to stir" (p. 342).

"I saw life," Buber says, "as the possibility of a dialogue with being." And Augie March is learning the language: "Occasionally, I could look out like a creature" (p. 345). Buber says, "An animal's eyes have the power to speak a great language . . . most forcibly when they rely wholly on their glance, the eyes express the mystery in its natural prison, the anxiety to becoming . . . there enters the glance a quality of amazement and inquiry."[23] Augie March is coming along: "The clouds, birds, cattle in the water, things . . . there was no need to herd, account for, hold them in the head, but it was enough to be among them, released on the ground as they were in their brook or in their air. . . . Creatures look out with their original eyes" (p. 345). Augie March is learning the language:

"Augie is the kind of person you ought to have," said Mimi, "somebody who can speak the workers' language."

It made me laugh to hear this advertised of me and I said I didn't know whose language I spoke (p. 301).

But we are beginning to know — and so is Augie. Augie March: torn, first, between the life of *It* and the life of *Thou*; directed to the latter by the feeling of "a great privation"; next, separating the daily life from holy; then, grudgingly accepting the necessity for the two to be taken together; and now, achieving moments where the sacred is seen in the commonplace, not as the concession but as triumph — Augie's education, though far from complete, is surely taking shape. He knows his occupation ("a sincere follower of love" [p. 417]); he knows that when he says Love he speaks of the transcendent ("If there was anything I knew by now it was how impossible it is to live without something infinitely mighty and great" [p. 429]); he does not know how to achieve his end. And thus, he is exactly like any Hasid — knowing that "All is God and all serves God . . . known in his longing, slumbering in germ in his ecstasy, and linked up in the rhythm of his actions."[24] "He must go out, yet does not know where it is to be found."[25]

Having reached this stage in his education, Augie demonstrates new understanding of several Hasidic principles: the redeemability of evil ("It seemed when somebody held me up an evil [the falcon] there had to be a remedy" [p. 363]); the rejection of reason as sole guiding light ("After much making with the sense, it's senselessness that you submit to" [p. 407]); the unique quality of the present ("the only possessing is of the moment" [p. 423]).

But Augie has a couple of important and difficult lessons left to learn. The first is what Buber calls "the exalted melancholy of our fate: that every *Thou* in our world must become an *It*."[26] The second and last — the final secret — is to learn that "the place where the treasure can be found is the place on which one stands," that the holy is there in the common hour, not by accident, but by design.[27]

Augie must learn that *Thou* passes, that it is not his fault. "What was the matter," he asks, feeling the wonder of Thea slipping away, "that pureness of feeling couldn't be kept up?" (p. 375). Later he says, "My real fault was that I couldn't stay with my purest feelings. This was what tore the greatest hole in me" (p. 418). And later still: "There was something wrong with me. I didn't love her as I ought to have. I should have been more pure" (p. 448). But Augie comes, in time, to accept this "exalted melancholy," this "sunrise and sunset of the spirit,"[28] as Buber calls it. And in retrospect, Augie explains it with Buberian sympathy: "It takes some of us a long time to find out what the price is of being in nature, and what the facts are about your tenure . . . from vast existence, in some way you rise up and at any moment you may go back. Any moment, the very next maybe" (p. 377).

But all things fall in place when the ultimate secret is learned — that "the great treasure, which may be called the fulfillment of existence, is found in the place where one stands."[29] The creature of ecstasy moves closer. In what amounts to a Hasidic parable Augie has a conversation about a classroom exercise:

> Mrs. Minsick was the teacher. She'd call you up to the front of the class and hand you a piece of chalk. "Now, Dorabella, what flower are you going to smell?" She'd say, "Sweetpea." . . . Stephanie Kriezcki, she'd say, "Violet, rose, nasturtium." Just catch the picture of this lousy classroom, and all these poor punks full of sauerkraut and bread with pig's feet, with immigrant blood and washday smells and kielbasa and home-brew beer. Where did they get off with this floral elegance? . . . Well, the wild kids would say, "Skunk cabbage, teach," or "Wild schmoo-flowers," or "Dreck." . . . Who ever saw any sweetpeas? . . . (p. 452).

Augie sees in the story two kinds of people ("Some stood up for what they knew and some longed for what they didn't." [p. 452]); the secret lies in the existence of a third — those who find flowers in sauerkraut. Now, Augie knows it cannot be right to find the washday smell miserable and so wallow in it: "It can never be right to offer to die, and if that's what the data of experience tell you, then you must get along without them" (p. 453). But having long ago decided not to die, Augie may yet offer to live. He may quit trying to smell sweetpeas in chalk and give himself up to the chalk itself.

Mimi knows the secret and she tells him. "The reason why I didn't see things as they are," Augie replies, "was that I didn't want to; because I couldn't love them as they were. But the challenge was not to better them in your mind but to put every human weakness into the picture — the bad, the criminal, sick, envious, scavenging, wolfish, the living on the dying. Start with that" (p. 453). And that is it exactly: to start there, to start loving there, to start redeeming there.

But this is no easy lesson to learn. The Hasid-picaro, the man of Holy Insecurity, must find his truth in the lived life; and when the world is nearly lost already to total *It*, it is that much more difficult. Still Augie encourages us. Our impatience for him to succeed ultimately is soothed by his minor successes, his understandings won on the way home. If Augie does not know exactly where that is, at least he knows where it is not: "The struggle of humanity," he says, "is to recruit others to your version of what's real. Then even the flowers and the moss on the stones become the moss and the flowers of a version. . . . The invented things never became real for me no matter how I urged myself to think they were" (p. 418). This version-making is precisely what Buber means when he says the man of *It*, "instead of freeing that which is bound up in the world . . . turns it to his own account. . . . When he saw it, it was nothing among things, no event among events, but exclusively present. Being did not share itself with him in terms of the law that was afterwards elicited from the appearance, but in terms of its very self." Buber, with Augie, decries a response to a flower that says, "This, then, is how the matter stands, the thing is called this, made in this way, its place is over there." The flower becomes an *It*, "used as *It*, appropriated for the undertaking to 'find one's bearing' in the world, and then to 'conquer it.' " [30]

And Bellow continues to cast across Augie's path the victims of this philosophy, the more palpably deprived products of the technical age. But now those champions of *It*, those who were before huge figures in the eyes of the protagonist, have been reduced in size by Augie's education. As Augie grows more and more to hallow his humanness, the two great manipulators, who treat others as things — Grandma Lausch and William Einhorn — steadily shrink into nothing. Once absolute dictator of the March home, attended by servants, her every word listened to with frightened concentration, Grandma Lausch is in the end carted off to an institution, shrunken from disregard, and brittle with pride. Einhorn, once seen amidst great wealth and space, a home of important concerns, and businesses spread before his wheelchair, is now to be found keeping an office in the corner of a pool hall. Now when Bellow introduces the philosophy of *It*, it is introduced without illusion. Robey, the addled philosopher, tells Augie, "I need advice . . . help," and speaks as if he were the age itself (p. 457). Robey, working on a "history of human happiness from the standpoint of the rich," wants to call his book "The Needle's Eye," "because there never had been a spiritual life for the rich if they didn't give up everything" (p. 458) — *and*, we suspect, because *no one*, Robey included, is going to get through this book. But the question with which Bellow teases himself and the reader is whether any of us, having come four hundred and fifty-eight pages ourselves, are going to make it through *his* book. Bellow continues the play within a play as he has Augie expound on Robey's ideas:

> Technology was going to create abundance and everyone would have enough of everything . . . the dream of the French Revolution coming to pass. But the French had been too optimistic and thought that when the decrepit old civilizations were busted nothing could stop us from entering the earthly paradise. But it wasn't so simple. We were facing the greatest crisis in history. And he didn't mean the war then coming on. No, we'd find out if there was going to be this earthly paradise or not. . . . "M-machinery'll make an ocean of commodities. Dictators can't stop it. Man will accept death. Live without God. That's a b-brave project. End of an illusion. But with what values instead? . . . But that's toward the end of the book" (p. 458).

Indeed, that's toward the end of the book — which we are fast approaching. Perhaps, as others have suggested, it is a flaw that Augie's final vision, his consummating ecstasy, appears to come out of nowhere, unprecedented by some important change.[31] But there is no flow. Buber would agree with Augie when he says, "any man at any time can come back to these axial lines . . . at any time life can come together again and man be regenerated" (p. 472). ("In each hour," Buber says, "in each act, in each speech the holy can blossom forth."[32]) Moreover, it seems to me, as I have tried to show here, that *everything* that has gone before has led Augie to this moment, this climax in a long and gradual education. And finally, there *is* some precession: a prayer, an incantory offering of self, such as the Hasidim say is essential to the letting in of God: "You are like me, a stranger on earth," the Hasid must finally say to his God, "and your indwelling has no resting place. So do not withdraw yourself from me, but disclose to me your commandment so that I can become your friend."[33] And Augie makes this prayer: "There was nothing that I longed for more than that. Let it come! Let there be consummation. . . . Let the necessity for the mystical great things of life, which, not satisfied, lives in us as the father of secret miseries, be fulfilled and have a chance to show it's not the devil himself" (p. 469). "God helps with his nearness," Buber says of this prayer, "the man who wants to hallow himself and his world." [34] "I was getting somewhere," Augie says moments later. "In fact I was lying on my couch in the state of grand summary one afternoon, still in my bathrobe and having called off all duties in the inspiration of the day . . . " (p. 470).

The grand summary, the conclusion of all that has gone before: the spirit is locked away by "opposition"; then it is released and seized upon at the exclusion of the daily life; in perverse order, the daily life is admitted to the spiritual, it is seen to pollute the spiritual; the two come together, fleetingly, but naturally, but indirectly; and now, finally, the resolution, the goal of the education, the only answer to *moha*, transcendence *in* the world:

> "I have a feeling," I said, "about the axial lines of life, with respect to which you must be straight or else your existence is merely clownery, hiding tragedy. I must have had a feeling since I was a kid about these axial lines which made me want to have my existence on them, and so I have said 'no' like a stubborn fellow to all my persuaders, just on the obstinacy of my memory of these lines, never entirely clear. But lately I have felt these thrilling lines again. When striving stops, there they are as a gift. I was lying on the couch here before and they suddenly went quivering right straight through me. Truth, love, peace, bounty, usefulness, harmony! And all noise grates, distortion, chatter, distraction, effort, superfluity, passed off like something unreal. And I believe that any

man at any time can come back to these axial lines, even if an unfortunate bastard, if he will be quiet and wait it out. The ambition of something special and outstanding I have always had is only a boast that distorts this knowledge from its origin, which is the oldest knowledge, older than the Euphrates, older than the Ganges. At any time life can come together again and man be regenerated, and he doesn't have to be a god or public servant like Osiris who gets torn apart annually for the sake of the common prosperity, but the man himself, finite and taped as he is, can still come where the axial lines are. He will be brought into focus. He will live with true joy. Even his pains will be joy if they are true, even his helplessness will not take away his power, even wandering will not take him away from himself, even the big social jokes and hoaxes need not make him ridiculous; even disappointment after disappointment need not take away his love. Death will not be terrible to him if life is not. The embrace of other true people will take away his dread of fast change and short life. And this is not imaginary stuff, Clem, because I bring my entire life to the test" (p. 472).

"I bring my entire life to the test": "Man should serve God," Buber writes, "with his whole strength, for all is needed."[35] Augie's vision is so aligned with Buber's understanding of what it is for a person to face the ultimate *Thou* — Buber and Bellow are here so illuminating of one another — that I quote at some length a few passages from *I and Thou*, which together speak to the dynamics of Augie's discovery:

> The ambition of something special and outstanding I have always had is only a boast that distorts this knowledge from its origin, which is the oldest knowledge, older than the Euphrates, older than the Ganges:

> *The relation to the* Thou *is direct. No system of ideas, no foreknowledge, and no fancy intervene between* I *and* Thou. *The memory itself is transformed, as it plunges out of its isolation into the unity of the whole. . . .*

> When striving stops, there they are as a gift:

No aim, no lust, and no anticipation intervene between I and Thou. Desire itself is transformed as it plunges out of its dream into the appearance. 36

. . . the man himself, finite and taped as he is, can still come where the axial lines are . . . even his helplessness will not take away his power:

Yes; in pure relation you have felt yourself to be simply dependent, as you are able to feel in no other relation—and simply free, too, as in no other time or place: you have felt yourself to be both creaturely and creative. You had the one feeling then no longer limited by the other, but you had both of them limitlessly and together. 37

And I believe that any man at any time can come back to these axial lines, even if an unfortunate bastard, if he will be quiet and wait it out:

The destiny of the relational event is here set forth in the most powerful way . . . Only silence before the Thou — silence of all tongues, silent patience in the undivided world that precedes the formed and vocal response — leaves the Thou free, and permits man to take his stand with it in the reserve where the spirit is not manifest, but is. 38

Something has just happened to me today:

What is the eternal, primal phenomenon, present here and now, of that which we term revelation? It is the phenomenon that a man does not pass, from the moment of the supreme meeting, the same being as he entered into it. The moment of meeting is not an "experience" that stirs in the receptive soul and grows to perfect blessedness; rather, in that moment something happens to the man. At times it is like a light breath, at times like a wrestling bout, but always—it happens. The man who emerges from the act of pure relation that so involves his being has now in his being something more than has grown in him, of which he did not know before and whose origin he is not rightly able to indicate . . . .

*Man receives, and he receives not a specific "content"
but a Presence, a Presence as power. This Presence and
this power include three things, undivided, yet in such a
way that we may consider them separately. First, there is
the whole fullness of real mutual action, of the being
raised and bound up in relation: the man can give no
account at all of how the binding in relation is brought
about, nor does it in any way lighten his life—it makes life
heavier, but heavy with meaning. Secondly, there is the
inexpressible confirmation of meaning. Meaning is
assured. Nothing can any longer be meaningless. The
question about the meaning of life is no longer there. But
were it there, it would not have to be answered. You do
not know how to exhibit and define the meaning of life,
you have no formula or picture for it, and yet it has
more certitude for you than the perceptions of your
senses. What does the revealed and concealed meaning
purpose with us, desire from us? It does not wish to be explained but only to be done by us. Thirdly, this meaning is
not that of "another life," but that of this life of ours, not
one of a world "yonder" but that of this world of ours and
it desires its confirmation in this life and in relation with
this world.* [39]

This is the climax of Augie's education. He does not ascend
to the heavens. He does not live out the remainder of his life in
enlightened bliss. He is not saved. But he does know. He
knows, as Buber says, "there is something that can only be
found in one place. It is a great treasure, which may be called
the fulfillment of existence. The place where this treasure can
be found is the place on which one stands." [40] "It is because
things happen but once," Buber says of *shiflut*, "that the
individual partakes in eternity." [41]

Most of us achieve only at rare moments a clear realiza-
tion of the fact that they have never tasted the fulfillment
of existence, that their life does not participate in true,
fulfilled existence, that, as it were, it passes true existence
by. We nevertheless feel the deficiency at every moment,
and in some measure strive to find—somewhere—what
we are seeking. Somewhere, in some province of the
world or of the mind, except where we stand, where we

have been set—but it is there and nowhere else that the treasure can be found. The environment which I feel to be a natural one, the situation which has been assigned to me as my fate, the things that happen to me day after day, the things that claim me day after day—these contain my essential task and such fulfillment of existence as is open to me.[42]

Augie March knows this now. His growth has been an education to ecstasy, to *hitlahabut*. He has grown to the awareness of how he can be fulfilled; and he has grown—if only for a moment—to fulfillment, to the place beyond ecstasy, *shiflut*, where one might "feel the universal generation as a sea and oneself as a wave." He is now the Hasid, living fully the life of Holy Insecurity, trying to re-achieve the moment of *Thou*: "My hope is based upon getting to be still so that the axial lines can be found" (p. 533). And he may make it and he may not. In any case, his posture in the world is certainly not one of accommodation. "He knows," as Buber says, knowing Augie so well, "that he must go out with his whole being . . . what is to come will come only when he decides on what he is able to will. He must sacrifice his puny, unfree will, that is controlled by things and instincts, to his grand will, which quits defined for destined being. Then he intervenes no more, but at the same time he does not let things merely happen. He listens to what is emerging from himself, to the course of being in the world."[43]

This is the new Augie, the educated Augie. The old Augie would have been swept away with Bateshaw's plan to "make every man a poet and every woman a Saint" (p. 528). The new Augie knows that you can and must be only who you are; and the new Augie knows that you must not "let things merely happen," but must listen to your true self. This Augie separates himself from this greatest of manipulators, this man who created a form of life that characterizes exactly the life of *It*: "living . . . but lacking two essential powers—the regenerative and the productive" (p. 524). Augie refuses Bateshaw: "No one will become a poet or saint because you fool with them. When you come right down to it, I've had trouble enough becoming what I already am, by nature" (p. 529). And fittingly, when Augie makes this declaration he is floating on a raft in the middle of the ocean, unsaved, a man of Holy Insecurity.

But whether or not he is ultimately saved, he is now the Hasid and he speaks like one: "Nobody should be a mystery intentionally. Unintentionally is mysterious enough" (p. 492). "It's secret over secret, mystery and then infinity sign stuck onto that. So who knows the ultimate, and where is the hour of truth?" (p. 501). He associates the simple with what he has learned: "My . . . special thing was simplicity. I wanted simplicity and denied complexity" (p. 418). He loves Minitouchian when he says, "How rare is simple thought and pureheartedness! Even a moment of pureheartedness I bow down to the ground" (p. 504). Speaking of *hitlahabut*, Buber says, "In its indivisible light all that was and that will be appears simple and united." [44]

"It wasn't so much education as love" (p. 534), Augie says of one of his own schemes perceptively, and perceptively of the scheme of this novel as well. Love is the only answer—the only answer for opposing the finite, he was told long ago. His education has been to learn what this means, to learn to answer: his world, himself, his own being. "I saw life," Buber says, "as the possibility of a dialogue with being." And Augie March, from beginning to end, is a person of possibilities.

"I want to suggest," Chester Eisenger has written, "that Bellow's basic attitudes—the overwhelming need for love and the joy in life—bear a remarkable similarity to the principles of Hasidism." [45] Apparently the first to have said this, Eisenger must be credited for his initial insight. Yet, his reading of *Augie March* seems a little unfortunate, and his appropriation of Hasidism more so. Having finished his discussion of *Augie March*, Eisenger writes, in *Fiction of the Forties*, "Bellow yet offers no evidence of either the theism or the mysticism characteristic of Hasidism. He is a secular Hasid, whether he knows it or not." [46]

Whether Eisenger knows it or not, every Hasid is a secular Hasid. The religion is practiced in the daily life, among "the things that claim me day after day." The Hasid's spiritual force is on the secular, on the *saeculum*, on—as Harvey Cox defines it—"this world and this time." [47] But aside from Eisenger's misunderstanding of Hasidism, he is wrong, too, I think, in saying *Augie March* is devoid of either theism or mysticism. Augie's long education has been a religious one, a search for something infinite and fulfilling; and in the course of that search there have been moments of consummate mystery. "Nobody should be a mystery intentionally. Unintentionally is mysterious enough."

Nor is it clear to me that Augie's moment of transcendence is somehow undercut, or diminished in value, as Keith Michael Opdahl argues, by the fact that it is not followed by satisfaction or in some way sustained.[48] I have said already that the Hasid lives in a state of Holy Insecurity; but, moreover, it seems to me that there is a sense in which Augie does return to his axial lines, even in the history of the novel: it is Augie after all who has "made the record." In telling the story in the way he has, Augie takes his place again in the world of *Thou*: "Said not in order to be so highly significant but probably because human beings have the power to say and ought to employ it at the proper time. When finally you're done speaking you're dumb forever after, and when you're through stirring you go still, but this is no reason to decline to speak and stir or to be what you are" (p. 539). "The primary word," Buber writes, "can only be spoken with the whole being. He who gives himself to it may withhold nothing of himself. The word does not suffer me . . . to relax in the world of *It*; but it commands. If I do not serve it aright it is broken or it breaks me."[49]

"He who gives himself to it may withhold nothing of himself." "If you hold down one thing," Augie says at the beginning, "you hold down the adjoining." Augie understands. He gives himself entirely—humanly. "Man cannot approach the divine by reaching beyond the human."[50] And as we watch Augie becoming human, we become more human ourselves. At the novel's beginning, when we stand with Augie in the wasteland, amidst the "answers of concession," and a low opinion of humankind, we wonder along with him when he says, "I wonder where in the creation there would be much of a double-take at the cry, '*Homo sum!*' " (p. 80). At the novel's end we merely wonder. Where in creation?—in Bellow's creation: here is a person to take another look at; here is a person who makes us take another look at ourselves. Augie, writing his record, is like Buber, writing his, and saying, "That God is, is to me almost less mysterious than that I am, I who write this with trembling fingers on a rock above a lake."[51]

Augie March, a man of ecstasy, of *hitlahabut*, Hasid, and hallower of the world around him: "I don't know who this saint was who woke up, lifted his face, opened his mouth, and reported on his secret dream that blessedness covers the whole Creation but covers it thicker in some places than in others. Who ever it was it is my great weakness to respond to such dreams. This is the *amor fati*, that's what it is, or mysterious adoration of what occurs" (p. 546).

We have met Augie and we leave him. And Buber, with his forceful reverence, says something of the feeling we take away from the experience: "That before which, in which, out of which, and into which we live, even the mystery, has remained what it was. It has become present to us as salvation; we have 'known' it, but we acquire no knowledge from it which might lessen or moderate its mysteriousness. We have come near to God, but no nearer to unveiling being or solving its riddle. We have felt release, but not discovered a 'solution.' We can only go and confirm its truth . . . we can, we *must*." [52]

farbrengen

*Today she is going to be dipped. It is earlier on a
Sunday than he remembers either of them getting up
in some time. All night, she tells him, she has been
dreaming of herself falling in muddy puddles unable
to keep herself clean for the bath. He tells her it reminds him of his mother preparing the house for the
cleaning lady. Be reminded of something else, she
tells him. Today she will complete several years of
preparation for conversion to Judaism. Today she
will become a new person. This he has his reserva-
tions about. He loved the one he met. Today, she
tells him, she will be born again. He cheers a little
for this Nazarene vestige, but silently; she wouldn't
know it for affection. He sees her bringing him the
Code of Jewish Law, the "Prepared Table." She reads
the passages on conversion. She is to be witnessed in
the ritual bath, and henceforth considered a new
person. Behold, it says, she is a Jewess in every
respect.*

*Her students are at the door, two friends she made
teaching high school, who happen to be Jewish. She
had asked them to witness the bath. Three
observant men, the law calls for. He does not qualify.*

*They drive to the bathhouse. When he learns
where it is — between Ida's Beauty Parlor and the
Cue 'N' Cushion — he is confronted with the first
vision of the much seen. He has been by this door
almost daily and never understood it. Now, in
Sunday's quiet, it stands between the plate glass
poverties of unattended pool tables and hair dryer
cavities, proclaiming itself, revealed. This kind of
moving to the fore, by standing still and letting the*

opposition step backward, he has much to learn about in the months ahead. For now it is enough to make his way inside. She has grown quiet.

Inside they find a friend and a stranger. The friend, Rick, a rabbinic assistant who brought her along in her studies, greets them buoyantly. His head covered, he hands skullcaps to the arriving men and introduces them to the president of the Mikvah Association. The man is shy at this title and shakes their hands and expresses happiness for her. The president says his name is David, and his wife takes her into the back. The men pace the cramped spaces of the waiting room, nervous, expecting the newborn.

In light of the general attitude toward mikvah — contempt too bitter not to be charged by fear — Rick understandably sought to prepare her weeks ago for the events of the present moment. Not knowing her well enough — which is to say, as well as he does — this served to place anxiety where there had been none, and a woman who minutes before could see nothing but religious excitement in a ritual bath observed by three observant men, now found the prospect nervous-making. Seeing things had not gone well, Rick promised her the ritual would be performed both according to Law and without male observers. This prospect excited Rick anyway, as he had been studying the Talmud on the matter and thought he saw a way to reconcile this contradiction. As for her, she had forgotten her anxiety the next day, never discussed the matter again with Rick, and, only a few days before, received a letter from the Mikvah Association in which the witnessing was referred to as "the height of modesty."

In the waiting room he is uncomfortable. He does not know how to behave. The occasion as he sees it

should be attended with light spirits and happy
hearts, but, mostly, there is hesitation. Too many
men on foreign ground. They are all taking looks at
the president of the Mikvah for clues, but he is un-
comfortable with them. And then, too, they are
crowded. Standing too close to each other to
maintain a personal space, five American men have
no options for intimacy — conversation is all that is
left to them. David, with soft awkwardness and a
gentle smile, asks him for the spelling of his name,
pronounces it, pursues it, and runs into his father,
who, it turns out, David is happy to say, helped him
once when he was learning accounting. This subject
runs out and they have need of another. He knows it
will be David again, shyer than all of them, who will
come up with it. It is his way of saying he is liking it
that they are here. A telephone is hanging on the
wall inches in front of David's nose and he finds a
story to tell about this. They pay close attention.
They hear giggling in the other room, first hers,
which is rich, easy, and familiar to her, then David's
wife's, also lovely, but in a different way, perhaps
because it is unaccustomed.

David smiles and stands in their space more inten-
tionally. David tells them that in a moment he and
Rick and one of the students will take a quick look
into the bath. Rick's response is too ready, too
Deuteronomic: "No, we won't do that. I forbid it,"
he says. David's face looks as if something has been
thrown into it. Rick explains that it is not necessary
for men to observe, that they can hear her in the
bath, that they know she is in there, that they can
ask David's wife. The president shrugs, his face and
shoulders huddling into unhappiness. "We have
always observed," he says, "that's how it's done."
Rick repeats himself, and mentions the names of

*local rabbis who concur with this conclusion. The
president is unimpressed by these rabbis; they are
not of the orthodox community. The president turns
toward a wall and looks far into space. They stand
silently, the air argumentative, their awkwardness
no longer benign.*

*"You don't see anything," the president says to
him, cryptically, then reminding them of their bath-
er. He glances at the document on the table waiting
for the signatures of the witnesses. Rick asks the
president what he is about to ask: "This won't give
you any difficulty in signing, will it?" Just hearing the
words he had been thinking, he realizes how silly
their question is. "Of course I can't sign," the man
says quietly, with disappointment. Now Rick is
angered; he mentions as further support an orthodox
rabbi the president respects. Stiffly the president
expresses doubt the rabbi would, in fact, sanction
such behavior. Rick says he would. The president is
angry. He pulls off the phone and dials. For an in-
stant, they see her robed, scampering out of the
back room into what must be a bathroom. David's
wife joins them and listening to her husband
speaking Yiddish on the phone, hears the story in a
version none of the others can verify. But they
understand the rabbi's response from the president's
face, and it is clear he has triumphed even before he
derisively calls Rick "Rabbi," handing him the
phone. Rick talks with the rabbi in English. Mean-
while David's wife is heard to say: "What's the
matter, I'm not a good enough witness? You won't
take my word for it?" Her face shows she is teasing
with this, mostly. He goes over to her when she
appears, dressed, radiant from the bathroom.*

*"I think she likes me," she whispers to him,
slipping her hands into his hands.*

"She's very nice," he says. "How was it?"

"Oh, wonderful; but I didn't say the blessing very well; she had to help me."

She is laughing and her eyelashes have tiny drops of water on them. Her skin is pink and she is wonderful to hold onto.

"But you didn't watch," she says, like an eight-year-old diver returning to poolside. She is very proud of herself.

Now he sees some confusion on her face as she gets a long look at the rest of the group.

"How would you like to go in again?" he asks her. "Rick's been protecting you out here, and there's been a mixup. It's all our fault, you're doing beautifully."

"I'd love to go in again," she says, still beaming at him, returning to the bathroom to disrobe.

He returns to the group and tries to explain why he would like to start over. This is not easy because he is not sure himself. It is not because he agrees or disagrees with either of the disputants. This he realized when he found himself attracted to David's reasoning that three witnesses are surely not persons who have heard from someone else that something has happened. He was attracted to this, and yet he saw no connection between it and the morning. Nor did he come to this decision out of displeasure with Rick or sympathy for David, since at the moment he liked them both and considered them both unpleasant. That brings him to her. He is struck not so much by the recognition that the others have left her to protect something they feel to be in greater danger as with the recognition he feels bound to protect her. This seems different than love, or later than love, or love. He suggests aloud that not everyone agrees that if they don't look it is legal, but everyone

agrees that if they do it is, and with that they make
their way — all five of them — to the door. He
deems himself as observant as the next man, and can
see no more than the top of her head. The bath is
vertical and four-walled, and the only way he knows
she is smiling is that he sees it in her eyes and he
hears her laughing. They close the door and turn
toward the witnesses' document and the weather
outside. He hears David's wife, laughing in answer
to her, laughing, this time more easily. He sends this
woman a message: you teach her your blessing and
she'll teach you hers.

Three French schoolgirls, a rabbi from Uruguay
who stayed in the lower half of the duplex next to
our own, two separate Israelis, a first chair violinist
in a London symphony, a hostess for Mobil Oil (it
meant she drove around the country inspecting rest-
rooms, she said), a boy from Italy, a Venezuelan I
had picked up at the airport myself, and a young
woman who came from California for a day and was
still waiting six days later. These were the out-of-
towners I saw in a single week who had come for a
meeting with the rebbe.

When I asked my chaver how they could come all
that way — one of the Israelis was there only two
days — he just said, "The man is a rebbe. People
come."

Once I heard that a woman in the community
came to see the rebbe, distraught.

"My son is just crazy." she said. "He wants to do
things he should not do. He wants to eat pig and
dance with girls."

"This does not sound crazy," the rebbe is said to
have replied. "Now, if he wanted to eat girls and
dance with pigs, that, I would say, was crazy."

HENDERSON THE RAIN KING: A FORM TO BURST THE SPIRIT'S SLEEP

Now, trumpeter, for thy close,
Vouchsafe a higher strain than any yet;
Sing to my soul — renew its languishing faith and hope;
Rouse up my slow belief — give me some vision
of the future;
Give me, for once, its prophecy and joy.[1]
— Walt Whitman

For soul is form, and doth the body make.[2]
— Edmund Spenser

Overdraw me Lord, and who cares if I break.[3]
— Nikos Kazantzakis

I have not, in previous chapters, considered in any detail the question of a novel's form. Although a perfectly legitimate literary exercise, such concern, it should be clear by now, lies generally outside, and at times contrary to, our attempt to commune with the inner pulse — the spirit — of the novel. "Spirit," Buber writes, "in its human manifestation, is a response of man to his *Thou*. . . . Spirit is not in the *I*, but between *I* and *Thou*."[4] The mystery of the universe is to be found not so much in its many, special, and separate parts, Buber suggests, as in the spaces between.

My concern is with *relation*. A discussion of form, as an end in itself, generally leads only to the realm of *experience*. I have no interest in approaching the novel to "experience what there is to be experienced," as Buber says, in order to learn that "it is made in this way, or this is expressed in it, or its qualities are such and such, and further it takes this place in the scheme of things."[5]

But there is an instance in which a discussion of form is not only relevant but necessary to our concerns. "It is not as though scientific and aesthetic understanding were not necessary," Buber says. They are necessary to the artist, for example, when they help him to "do his work with precision and to plunge it into the truth of relation — relation which is above the understanding, which gathers understanding up in itself" — the relation of *I* and *Thou*.[6] *Henderson the Rain King*, crazy and outrageous, is a formal novel. It is a novel of and about form. Its creator and its protagonist both seek a form to help them plunge into the truth of relation, transcending understanding, to meet the spirit.

Neither the novel nor the protagonist compose forms finally that take their place in the world of *It*, waiting to be measured, their qualities recordable. Rather they seek and become forms that are finally beyond measure: "Life may think it has got me written off in its records," says our hero at one point. "Henderson: type so and so . . . illustrating such-and-such a principle, and laid aside. But life may find itself surprised, for after all, we are men. I am Man — I myself, singular as it may look. Man. And man has many times tricked life when life thought it had him taped."[7] And the novel, too, seeking and finding the form of the myth — where, through the worldly, man reaches the soul — finally goes beyond measure itself. It will be through our examination of this dual quest for form that we will try to meet once again the mystery of the spaces between.

In voice, setting, character, and plot, *Henderson* reigns, the most fully pursued novel of Bellow's career. Eugene Henderson, an older Augie, knows from the beginning of the axial lines: his "cloud of glory," he says at the end, he may have abused for most of his life, but "I always knew what it was" (p. 285). If Henderson knows better, so does Bellow as well; and if the internal spirit shapes the body outside (as the African King Dahfu will suggest) we know better ourselves where one book surpasses the other.

If *Augie March* announced a completely new American voice in the literature of this century, *Henderson* established it. Where Augie's indirection is compounded by the author's own, the voice of gigantism runs away with itself, until Augie's words, "I could have benefited from the wisdom that the heavy is the root of the light . . . that the graceful comes out of what is buried at great depth" (p. 317), serve as a sighing reappraisal by a now older author, possessed of the wisdom and able to put it to use in his later work. In *Henderson the Rain King*, the light has risen out of Augie's heaviness, and Bellow flowers, drawing on old roots to gain a distinctly American grace.

"The Jews are perhaps the only people," Buber says, "that never ceased to produce myth."[8] In another place he says, "Experience which has taken place (not 'been gained') in factual encounters with the world and the soul, is directly embodied in myth."[9] And it is through the election of myth, of fable, that Bellow gains his American grace, finds a more controllable vessel for his tone of voice, in the creation of his mythical protagonist. The tone of gigantism, of near-gluttonous ingathering, of conspicuous verbal consumption — of America — comes to us as much in the shape of this bumbling Bunyan as in the shape of the novel itself. Given this twenty-two-inch neck through which to do his bellowing, this kisser of life with denture problems, this man full of money, full of children — this America — Bellow is more successful with the overwriting, flailing, and finally self-mocking voice he first introduces in *Augie March*. Where earlier it was the novel itself that occasionally flailed and seemed to be mocked, here the fury comes from the character alone, more largely achieved, living in a form that never appears in *Augie March*

We will see, then, how the mythic form can give the Bellow voice a better hearing. How does it influence setting, character, and plot? The simplification that Augie March so passionately seeks in his own story is employed in the telling of Henderson's "living proof of something of the highest importance." "All positive religion" — this from Buber again — "depends upon an immense simplification in all that in the world and in our souls presses on us so inextricably and so importunately; it is the taming and subjugation of the fullness of existence. . . . *Mythos* is the expression of this fullness of existence, its image and its mark."[10] By taking Henderson "far, far" back into the past — "the real past, no history or junk like that. The prehuman past" (p. 42) — by "penetrating beyond geography" until environment is mystery itself, Bellow reduces the space of his canvas while plunging it to greater depths — thus pursuing the more positive directions of *Augie March* while eliminating the problem of its unwieldiness. The way in which myth influences Bellow's particular use of characters seems to be admirably described by R. P. Blackmur, who, in another context entirely, writes of the "dialectic of incarnation."[11] This trope refers to an artist's use of his characters, their reactions and responses, as an incarnation of "a force greater than ourselves, outside ourselves, and working on ourselves, which whether we call it God or Nature is the force of life, what is shaped or misshaped, construed or misconstrued, in the process of living."[12] Using his characters in this way, the artist hopes "to approach the conditions of rebirth, the change of heart, or even the fresh start."[13]

In the same article, Blackmur's words on plot are relevant to the form and function of the novel's action. "The great business of the novel," he says, speaking with what we will see is a remarkable directness to the novel at hand, "is to create out of manners and action motive, and out of the conflict of the created motive . . . to find the significance: an image of the theoretic form of the soul."[14]

I am suggesting, then, that Bellow's use of myth, influencing voice, setting, character, and plot, at once invests the novel with more form, more structure, and more control than *Augie March*, while at the same time puts it in more constant touch with the formless, the unstructured, and the uncontrolled — with the mysteries.

What motive emerges from the manners and action of Eugene Henderson, seven times a father, thrice a millionaire, twice a husband?: "A ceaseless voice in my heart that said, *I want, I want, I want, oh, I want*" (p. 14). Having plenty of size, plenty of money, plenty of women, plenty of children, Henderson finally has nothing he wants — and a voice to constantly remind him. It is Henderson's education in the novel to learn what part of him is doing this talking; it is his grace and good fortune to be able in the end to satisfy its demands. And it is his inability to answer this "demand that consumed my heart," this "terrible repetition within" that causes Henderson to act as he does prior to his departure for Africa. He gets drunk and picks fights. He gets drunk and spends his days smashing bottles at a fancy resort ("they accept no Jews and then they get me"[p. 10]). He gets drunk and runs himself over in a tractor. "Temper, vanity, rashness and all the rest," he says later. "These things occupy the place where a man's soul should be" (p. 73). Throughout all this "a voice spoke that said, *I want, I want, I want!* . . . And I would ask, 'What do you want?' But this was all it would ever tell me. It never said a thing except *I want, I want, I want!* . . . No purchase, no matter how expensive, would lessen it. Then I would say, 'Come on, tell me. What's the complaint, is it Lily herself? Do you want some nasty whore? It has to be some lust . . .' " (pp. 24 - 25).

Henderson may not know at this point what it is he wants, what it is he needs, but the pitch of the tension is already established: the day of spiritual rebirth is sighted from afar: "There comes a day," Henderson says, "there always comes a day of tears and madness" (p. 24). "For who shall abide the day of His (the rightful one's) coming? And who shall stand when He (the rightful one) appeareth?" (p. 32). "The soul driven round in this dizzy whirl," Buber writes, "cannot remain fixed within it, it strives to escape." [15] "Myth," Northrup Frye writes in *Anatomy of Criticism*, "is the imitation of actions near or at the conceivable limits of desire." [16]

Henderson's voice, *I want, I want,* seeks the fulfillment of the spirit, expresses what the Hasids call the "inner urge." "The greater a person is, so much greater is his urge," say the Hasids, justly measuring our protagonist. "From the greatness of the temptation a soul recognizes how holy it is in its roots." [17] In answering the urge, "a decision takes place in each man and on it redemption depends." [18] "Everyone has in him something precious that is in no one else," Buber writes. "But this precious something in a man is revealed to him only if he truly perceives his strongest feeling, his central wish, that in him which stirs his inmost being." [19] It is not until Henderson is deep in Africa — Inmost Being, dark confusion, primitive possibility having themselves become geography, having become setting — that he perceives his central wish. "In many cases," Buber goes on, "a man knows his strongest feeling only in the shape of a particular passion, of the 'Evil Urge' which seeks to lead him astray."[20]

In the beginning Henderson is led astray. But there is never any doubt that he has the grace. Henderson is no accommodator; he is a kisser of life. In a wonderful episode, Bellow tells of Clara Spohr (spore?), now in her sixties, "supposed to have been a famous beauty, and has never recovered from the collapse of this, but dresses like a young girl with flounces and flowers" (p. 108). Clara is the wife of the painter doing Lily Henderson's portrait, and one day, after meeting accidentally, Henderson goes home with Clara to pick up his wife. On the ride to her home "Clara was burning," Henderson tells us. "She talked and talked and worked on me with her eyes and her turned up nose. You could see the old mischief working, the life-craving, which wouldn't quit" (p. 109). Clara tells Henderson about the passionate love experiences of her youth, and when they reach her door, he, like a gentleman, leans to assist this sixty-six-year-old woman with her galoshes. "With a cry she lifted me up by the face and began to kiss me . . ." (p. 110). And Henderson kisses her back, not dutifully but mightily, "as if the next moment we were going to be separated by the stroke of death . . . I was not passive. I tell you, I kissed back" (p. 110). This Henderson is a man of grace, an embracer, a kisser of life in whatever form life may take.

Henderson, in the beginning, may be wallowing; he may be led astray. But there comes a day of tears and madness, the dark night of the soul, the dizzy whirl. Henderson knows:

> There is a curse on this land. There is something bad going on. Something is wrong. . . . Oh, shame, shame. Oh, crying shame! How can we? Why do we allow ourselves? What are we doing? The last little room of dirt is waiting. Without windows. So for God's sake make a move, Henderson, put forth effort. You, too, will die of this pestilence. Death will annihilate you and nothing will remain, because nothing will have been and so nothing will be left. While something still *is* — now! For the sake of all get out (pp. 36 - 37).

"We should receive this appearance and do what it demands of us," Buber writes. "In the sphere of our fantasy liberate the pure passion from its object which limits it, and direct it to the limitless." [21] Bellow creates out of his fantasy, liberates the passion, sends Henderson into the jungle to meet the limitless: "I was entering the past — the real past, no history or junk like that. The prehuman past." "I'm still not convinced I didn't penetrate beyond geography" (p. 50). "It must be older than the city of Ur" (p. 43).

Henderson is not long in the jungle before we discover indeed he has known all along about his "cloud of glory." Having before related only to pigs, he now "lays on the ground, the face of the air breathing back on us, breath for breath" (p. 43). "And I believed that there was something between the stones and me," he says (p. 42). At the completion of his interview with the woman of Bittahness — a scene we will return to in a moment — Henderson is visited by the inexorable wave of life, which celebrates with him their reunion. Sitting in a cave, wearing nothing much more than a loincloth, chewing a ham — here amid the origin and primacy of the first cavefolk: Henderson notices "the light at daybreak against the white clay of the wall beside me." It "had an extraordinary effect, for right away I began to feel the sensation in my gums warning of something lovely, and with it a close or painful feeling in the chest, . . . I felt the world sway under me and I would have reached, if I were on a horse, for the horn of the saddle" (p. 86). As does Buber in his vision of the sun upon a maple twig, Henderson makes contact with the mystery of his universe in the everyday hour. "Again and again," it is written in *I and Thou*, "that which has the status of object must blaze up into presentness and enter the elemental state from which it came, to be looked on and lived in the present by men." [22] Bellow does not hesitate to endow the moment with the supernatural: "Some powerful magnificence, not human, in other words, seemed under me," Henderson says. "I had known these moments when the dumb begins to speak, when I hear the voices of objects and colors; then the physical universe starts to wrinkle and change and heave and rise and smooth, so it seems that even the dogs have to lean against a tree, shivering" (p. 87).

Anxious that the moment will pass too quickly, Henderson seeks to draw out every ounce of the mystery, kneeling before it, pressing his face against the wall. But pass it must, the exalted melancholy of our fate; and Henderson, aware that this is so, "let it go without a struggle, hoping it would come again before another fifty years had passed" (p. 88).

Thus Henderson, attuned to the axial lines, knowing the *Thou*, accepting its transiency, must undergo a form of education far in advance of Augie March. This kind of an experience comes at the climax of Augie's education. Buber claims, for example, that one characteristic of this "eternal, primal meeting," is "the phenomenon that a man does not pass from the moment of the supreme meeting, the same being as he entered into it." [23] Augie does not feel this until the end of his story. [24] Henderson knows it early in Africa: "I was a different person, or thought I was. I had passed through something, a vital experience" (p. 88). Where it is Augie's conclusion at the end of a long step-by-step approach to the truth that the holy is to be found in the everyday, Henderson is in touch with the reality practically from the outset. Augie concludes at the end of his story that "blessedness covers the whole creation," and that he lives with an *amor fati*, or a "mysterious adoration of what occurs" (p. 546). Henderson has these same feelings from the beginning: "I have always argued that Lily neither knows nor likes reality. Me? I love the old bitch just the way she is and I like to think I am always prepared for even the very worst she has to show me. I am a true adorer of life. And if I can't reach as high as the face of it, I plant my kiss somewhere lower down. Those who understand will require no further explanation" (p. 128).

Hence Henderson's quest goes beyond Augie's. And in what way? Henderson's search is for a definition, a size, a shape, a form — a search, as Blackmur says, for "an image of the theoretic form of the soul"; but a form, as Buber says, "which is above understanding," a form to plunge us into deepest relation. The search is for a form of the soul, and if it is to be found, tangible and visible, it is a search that can only go on in a world quite different from our own. "Form is disclosed to the artist," Buber writes, "as he looks at what is over against him." [25] It is the artist's response, in other words, to the mystery. Myth is the form disclosed to Bellow, for it is the only form with which to capture so directly, so humanly, an image of the soul of man. When Henderson approaches the woman of Bittahness he is in the presence of *Thou* incarnate, the holy-space-between come to life, "a Be-er," Henderson says later, "if ever there was one."

The form of greeting among the Arnewi embodies the *I-Thou* relationship, as each puts his hand on the heart of the other, running pulse into pulse to say hello. "There was the calm pulsation of her heart," Henderson says, participating in the introduction. "This was as regular as the rotation of the earth . . . as if I were touching the secrets of life" (p. 63). When he kisses her stomach, to respond to the Bittah's like gesture of affection, Henderson feels that he has "made contact with a certain power." Who is this woman of Bittahness? As Itelo explains it, she is the African's answer to the *zaddik*, the Hasidic leader, a person on the highest rung: "She had risen above ordinary human limitations. . . . You couldn't be any higher or better" (p. 65).

In the ensuing dialogue, Henderson is painfully reminded of the distance that separates him from the Bittah, from an apprehension of his true being. "Who am I," Henderson thinks,

> a millionaire wanderer and wayfarer? A brutal and violent man driven into the world . . . a fellow whose heart said, *I want, I want?* Who played the violin in despair, seeking the voice of angels. Who had to burst the spirit's sleep or else. . . . That I had ruined the original piece of goods issued to me and was travelling to find a remedy? Or that I had read somewhere that the forgiveness of sin was perpetual but with typical carelessness had lost the book? (p. 63).

Henderson is looking for the book, for a form to burst the spirit's sleep, for the shape of an announcement that "creation," as Buber says, "does not merely take place once in the beginning but also at every moment throughout the whole of time."[26] He sees the Bittah as a source of salvation: "I believed the queen could straighten me out if she wanted to; as if, any minute now, she might open her hand and show me the thing, the source, the germ, the cipher. The mystery, you know" (p. 69).

But what the Bittah—being being incarnate—shows Henderson, fittingly enough, is himself: "You have, sir, a large personality. Strong. . . . Possess some fundamental of Bittahness, also. . . . You are very sore, oh sir! Mistah Henderson. You heart is barking. . . . Grun-tu-molani. Says you want to live. Grun-tu-molani. Man want to live" (pp. 72 - 74). And Henderson exalts in this insight, which he is to carry with him for the remainder of his journey. "I molani for myself," he says. "And I molani for everybody. I could not bear how sad things have become in the world and so I set out because of this molani. . . . God does not shoot dice with our souls . . ." (p. 74). "The world is not divine sport," Buber has said, "it is divine destiny."[27]

And Henderson, answering his destiny, sets out to find the measure of his spirit: "Every man feels from his soul that he has got to carry his life to a certain depth. Well, I have to go on because I haven't reached that depth yet" (p. 91). Henderson searches for a form, but, in truth, it is a form beyond measure, that form which Buber discusses, beyond understanding, the form of the spirit, the form that is the essence of human being. Henderson will not allow himself to be seen as any measurable form, a thing, an *It*, with recordable characteristics: "Life may think it has got me written off in its records. . . . But life may find itself surprised, for after all we are men. I am Man. And man has many times tricked life when life thought it had him taped."

But Henderson's visit with the Arnewi results in the bursting not of his spirit's sleep but of the village's cistern. The attempt to rid the water supply of its frogs is an episode that mirrors the entire book, in that it combines the hilarious with the formal. The scene, of course, gives us a greater insight into Henderson's personality—how enormous is his need to be of help, to make contact with people—and how enormously he stumbles on the job. But we have had this insight, though perhaps not so riotously, several times before. It is all drawn so largely, so gigantically produced, that we must ask ourselves why Bellow has included it. The function of the episode is, I think, a purely formal one. True to the pattern of a myth or fable, the hero must seek the Grail, seem to attain it, and then fail utterly, falling to abysmal depths, from which we do not think it possible for him or her ever to recover. Only then, having touched victory and seen it slip through his or her grasp, can the hero go on to true and final triumph. Thus Henderson cannot, at this stage, break the spell on himself or the Arnewi. The drought continues and the hero moves on.

Unable to find his soul among a good and friendly tribe, he is taken into custody by the Wariri — "dem chillen dahkness" — and immediately feels himself to be offered a vision of what he is looking for. Thrown into a tent with a dead man, he hears the body saying, "Here, man, is your being, which you think so terrific." To which Henderson answers, "Oh, be quiet, dead man, for Christ's sake" (p. 117). No, being is not a dead man, but the dead man brings Henderson closer to being. "What if this man should turn out to be a Lazarus?" he thinks. "I believe in Lazarus. I believe in the awakening of the dead. I am sure that for some, at least, there is a resurrection" (p. 119). Thus the dead man becomes Henderson himself, a Lazarus whose spirit sleeps and yearns to be awakened. (King Dahfu later says he believes Henderson has in him a "touch of the Lazarus" [p. 252]). In the myth, Frye says, we find "a world of total metaphor, in which everything is potentially identical with everything else, as though it were all inside a single infinite body."[28] Strong enough to bear the enormous weight of the man, Henderson suggests his own resurrectability, as he lifts up the corpse and carries him out of the tent. "Why you mus?" asks Romilayu, his man Friday, when the feat is still in the planning stages. "Because I just must," Henderson answers. "It's practically constitutional with me" (p. 118). Later he says he was "determined as only a man can be who is saving his life" (p. 119). As a figure of evil the body also suggests that aspect of the spirit with which Henderson has yet to deal. In the background, throughout the scene, we hear the steady roar of a lion. The episode has about it the feeling of initiation, and we are later to learn that in lifting up the body and carrying it on his back, Henderson, in effect, begins his education—an education that will lead him to that relation Buber celebrates and an image of the theoretic form of the soul.

Immediately following his ordeal with the corpse, Henderson wins admission to the palace and an audience with the man who is to lead him to salvation—the young king, Dahfu. Henderson, as we have seen, is well aware of his holy sparks. They pound inside him, begging *I want, I want,* begging for release; it is escape that they want. But Henderson cannot release them. "Such is the slavery of the times," he says, and though he refers to his own taciturnity, he seems to be speaking of the sparks as well: "I often want to say things and they stay in my mind. Therefore they don't exist; you can't take credit for them if they never emerge" (p. 149). You can't take credit for your holy sparks if they remain entrapped. The mystery of the holy is to be found not in the many, special, and separate parts of the universe, but in the spaces between. The sparks are released in the relationship of an *I* to a *Thou*. Bellow's dark, primal jungle is the perfect setting for that relationship, and King Dahfu is the man who helps Henderson burst his spirit's sleep. "There was something about this man," Henderson says, upon first meeting Dahfu, "that gave me the conviction we could approach ultimates together" (p. 132).

And ultimately this is precisely what occurs. Although at the outset we do feel the relationship is one-sided, by the time the story ends, we see clearly that it is perfectly mutual, mythically natural, that in Henderson, Dahfu too, finds salvation.

In the beginning, however, Henderson is a student of the King. Our hero sets up an enduring dichotomy between "being people" and "becoming people" and he is quite sure where he and the King should be placed respectively:

> Some people found satisfaction in *being* (Walt Whitman: "Enough to merely be! Enough to breathe! Joy! Joy! All over joy!"). *Being*. Others were taken up with *becoming*. Being people have all the breaks. Becoming people are very unlucky, always in a tizzy. The Becoming people are always having to make explanations or offer justifications to the Being people. . . . Now Willatale, the Queen of the Arnewi, and principal woman of Bittahness, was a Be-er if ever there was one. And at present, King Dahfu. If I had really been capable of the alert consciousness which it required I would have confessed that Becoming was beginning to come out of my ears. Enough! Enough! Time to have Become. Time to Be! Burst the spirit's sleep. Wake up America. Stump the experts (p. 135).

The goal of *kavana* is "redemption, that the soul shall return home from its exile. . . . To many a Hasid," Buber says, "it is, for the whole of his life, as if this must happen here and now. For he hears the voice of becoming roaring in the gorges and feels the seed of eternity in the ground of time as if it were in his blood. And so he can never think otherwise than that *this* moment and now *this* one will be the chosen moment. And his imagination compels him ever more fervently, for ever more commandingly speaks the voice and ever more demandingly swells the seed." [29]

As the mutuality of the relationship begins to evidence itself, Dahfu shows that he, too, is a man of becoming; but here
in the beginning, Henderson is the student and Dahfu is the
teacher. The subject?: "higher things," "the noumenal
department": "The world of facts is real, all right, and not to
be altered. The physical is all there, and it belongs to science.
But then there is the noumenal department, and there we
create and create and create. . . . I am ignorant and untutored
in higher things—in higher things I am a coarse beginner,
because of my abused nature—I didn't know what to expect"
(p. 142).

Dahfu's influence first begins to show its effect at the tribal
ceremony—the climax of which is "the flowing of the
heavens," the offering from "the pumps of the firmament," the
coming of rain—and, finally, the coronation of Henderson as
the Rain King.[30]

Henderson's response to the King's teaching is to have
awakened within him the notion of a possible form: "The King
himself had shown me the way . . . for instance, that chaos
doesn't run the whole show. That this is not a sick and hasty
ride, helpless, through a dream into oblivion. No, sir! It can be
arrested by a thing or two. By art, for example. The speed is
checked, the time is redivided. Measure! That great thought.
Mystery!" (p. 149).

Moments after this, Henderson yearns to embrace a form of
this mystery; he yearns to embrace a god—the half-ton statue
in the middle of the arena that must be moved from one spot
to another in order for the rain to commence. Spurred on,
subtly, by his redeemer, the King, Henderson's spirit stands
ready to burst. Our hero's condition is one of *hitlahabut*,
Hasidic ecstasy, fervor leading man to God: "I burned to go
out there and do it. Craving to show what was in me, burning
like that bush I had set afire . . . in the process . . . should my
heart be ruptured, should the old sack split, okay, then let me
die. . . . So inflamed was my wish to *do* something. I was excited to the bursting point. I swelled, I was sick, and my blood
circulated peculiarly through my body—it was turbid and
ecstatic both" (pp. 157 - 158).

His relationship to the events of the festival takes on finally
the intensity of an *I* to a *Thou*—consorting with the mysteries
in relation:

I knew. I heard it. The silent speech of the world to which

my most secret soul listened continually now came to me with spectacular clarity. Within—within I heard. Oh, what I heard! The first stern word was *Dummy!* I was greatly shaken by this. And yet there was something there. It was true. And I was obliged, it was my bounden duty to hear. *And nevertheless you are a man. Listen! Harken unto me, schmohawk! You are blind. The footsteps were accidental and yet the destiny could be no other. So now do not soften, oh no, brother, intensify rather what you are. This is the one only ticket—intensify. Should you be overcome, you slob, should you lie in your own fat blood senseless, unconscious of nature whose gift you have betrayed, the world will soon take back what the world unsuccessfully sent forth. Each peculiarity is only one impulse of a series from the very heart of things—that old heart of things. The purpose will appear at last though maybe not to you* (p. 159).

Only moments before he enters the arena, Henderson manifests a relationship to the four Hasidic stances. Hungering for *shiflut* ("I had a great desire to do a disinterested and pure thing—to express my belief in something higher"), crazed by intention ("I had got caught up in the thing, and it had regard only to the unfinished business of years—*I want, I want*"), looking to serve ("There is some kind of service motivation which keeps on after me"), ecstatically aflame ("But anyway, that burning, that craving, that flowing estuary—you see what I mean?"), he lifts up the god. She is, to him, "not an idol," but a "living personality," "a living old woman" (p. 163). "We met," Henderson says, "as intimates." The feat performed, rain on the way, Henderson attains a kind of peace, described in much the same way Augie March describes his alignment with the axial lines. "My spirit was awake and it welcomed life anew," he says. And it is to Dahfu, with whom his relationship is now about to "intensify," that he extends his gratitude. "'Thanks to you,'" he says, "'for giving me such a wonderful chance. Not just hoisting up the old woman, but to get into my depth. That real depth. I mean the depth where I have always belonged.' I was grateful to him. I was his friend then. In fact, at this moment, I loved the guy" (p. 164).

Having found a friend — and a form — to take him to this

depth, Henderson now must work at this depth for the ultimate discovery — the theoretic shape of his own soul. And this work goes on, of course, within the context of relationship—his relationship to the King. The order of their dealings with one another is immediately set at an important level: " 'You want to do me a favor, Your Highness? The biggest possible?' 'Assuredly. Why certainly.' 'All right, then, this is it: Will you expect the truth from me? That's my only hope. Without it everything else might as well go bust' " (p. 179).

Dahfu, in accord with this request, answers in terms of form or shape: "But do you have expectation," Dahfu says, "as to the form the truth is to take? Are you prepared if it comes in another shape, unanticipated?"

Henderson responds that he is prepared, and the relationship quickly moves to investigate the place of evil in the soul—something with which Henderson has not yet come to grips. Their dialogue presents two views of evil, in line with the dual interpretation of Hasidism, which Buber says exists "in the manner of two stages or steps of a process." [31] The names Buber gives to these two stages are very close to Henderson's own formulation (being and becoming): Buber calls them "the becoming-like-God stage," and "the being-like-God stage." [32] And ultimately, what the two stages represent is the process whereby man enters into relationship. In the first position evil is merely the lowest rung on the "ladder of good"; evil is that part of the spirit which waits to be redeemed; until the individual reaches the highest rung, the eternal *Thou*, evil will remain a part of the whole. It is this position, the "becoming-like-God" position, that Dahfu first has in mind when he explains that man, by his nature, inflicts misery on his fellowman. "Wait a minute," Henderson says. "You say the soul will die if it can't make somebody else suffer what it suffers?" Dahfu answers, "For a while, I am sorry to say . . ." (p. 181). This is the "becoming" phase of relationship, and Dahfu and Henderson illustrate it perfectly. At this stage persons respond to one another in terms of use. Dahfu, as we later come to see quite starkly, literally has to make Henderson suffer what he suffers if his soul is not to die. This is the stage of the *I-It* relationship. Dahfu says as much, though at this point Henderson does not realize how largely he has been used: "We could not refrain from making use of you," the King says. "It was because of the circumstances. You will pardon me" (p. 183). In this stage man resists what is holy, fighting the gods and his godliness: "Is this why me and the gods had to be beaten?" (p. 181) Henderson asks. But Henderson insists on another placement for evil, and this, of course, is the second stage in the process. Here we have not the redemption from evil but the redemption of evil; the evil impulse is sublimated into the *I-Thou* relationship. Dahfu naturally accepts this position, for his full answer to Henderson's first question is, "For a while I am sorry to say [the soul will die if it can't make another suffer], *it then feels peace and joy*" (p. 181).

"There are some guys," Henderson says, arguing the Hasidic position forcefully, "who can return good for evil." This, Hasidism says, is the end of the process, and Dahfu explains it as such: "You are right," he says, "for the long run; and good exchanged for evil truly is the answer. . . . I think the noble will have its turn in the world" (p. 181).

This understood, Dahfu and Henderson embark on a project to sublimate the evil impulse, to plunge their relationship to the depths of *Thou*, that each may save the other. Henderson says of his feelings for Dahfu: "Human perfections are shortlived, and we love them more than we should, maybe. But I couldn't help it. The thing was involuntary. I felt a pang in my gums, where such things register themselves without my will and then I knew how I was affected by him." "Without reserve," Dahfu answers, "I am developing a similar attitude toward you" (p. 182).

Henderson asks the King just how the noble is going to have its turn: "I mean what practical approach do you recommend?" he says. And Dahfu answers that he does in fact have "a conception about it" (p. 182); that he is "most eager to advance it to you."

Almost immediately the two make the descent into the palace's darkest regions. "Have faith," Henderson says to himself, frightened by this turn of events. "It's about time you had some faith" (p. 186).

Having pledged to accept reality—the truth, life—in whatever form it may take, Henderson finds himself face to face with Dahfu's lion. "It is a cruelly dangerous enterprise," Buber writes, "this becoming a whole, becoming a form, this crystallization of the soul." [33] Although frightened almost beyond consciousness, Henderson realizes, at this first meeting, the presence of the Mysteries. Of Dahfu he notes that "in every moment of his earthly life the extra shadow of brilliance was with him—the sign of an intenser gift of being" (p. 189). He says he thought he might pass out, more because of "rapture" than fear—"the richness of the mixture." Foremost in his mind is "the hour that bursts the spirit's sleep" (p. 190).

After this first session the two move closer together, as Henderson tells Dahfu of the incessant voice crying within him. And Dahfu, quite taken with this disclosure, answers quickly in the spirit of Hasidic dialogue: "It will persist until you have replied," he says. To this end Dahfu engages Henderson in extended conversations, and forces him to visit regularly with the lion.

In conversation, Dahfu discloses his theory that the form of the person is shaped by the spirit inside. In a novel of and about form, this theory has much to say to us. Its origins can be traced to Emerson (and from him to Spenser [34]), Romanticism having much in common with Hasidism. "The soul makes the body," Emerson says in "The Poet," and Bellow's emphasis of the idea reminds us that the ultimate "theoretic shape of the soul" is to be Henderson himself. Six and a half feet tall, twenty-two inches around the neck, Henderson becomes Bellow's dedication, for all its outrageousness, to the awesome dimensions of the soul.

To make Henderson recognize his fullest dimension, Dahfu confronts him continually with the lion. "But why a lion?" Henderson asks himself. "Because," he answers, "you don't know the meaning of true love if you think it can be deliberately selected. You just love, that's all. A natural force. Irresistible" (p. 217). And irresistibility is one of the qualities the King tries to get Henderson to see in the lion — to see in the human soul. "She is unavoidable," he says. "And this is what you need, as you are an avoider. Oh, you have accomplished momentous avoidances. But she will change that. She will make consciousness to shine. She will burnish you. She will force the present moment upon you" (p. 219). "The present," as Buber has told us before, "arises only in virtue of the fact that the *Thou* becomes present. The real, filled present, exists only in so far as actual presentness, meeting, and relation exist." [35] This is the great quality Dahfu sees in the lion — its power to force relation: "When she gives her tail a flex it strikes against my heart" (p. 219).

Henderson, his soul a victim of "the slavery of the times,"

must be forced to confront the lion and himself. "The tendency of your conscious is to isolate self" (pp. 224 - 225) Dahfu tells him. In order to end his alienation between the self and the spirit, Dahfu has Henderson get down on all fours, exhorts him to roar, to imitate the king of the jungle. Henderson balks at this, finds it enormously difficult. "Until the soul as form has such great power over the soul as matter," Buber writes, "until chaos is subdued and shaped into cosmos, what an immence resistance!" But finally the sound comes out, the road is reopened between spirit and self: "I gave myself to it, and all my sorrow came out in the roaring. My lungs supplied the air but the note came from my soul" (p. 225).

And Henderson's relationship with Dahfu intensifies, by definition, at the same pace as Henderson's approach to the lion. When Henderson balks at Dahfu's requests concerning the lion, Dahfu makes it clear that Henderson is resisting the intensifying of their relationship as well. "I am close to you," Dahfu says. "But I require more deep relationship. I desire to be understood and communicated to. We have to develop an underlying similarity which lies within you by connection with the lion" (p. 218). The lion, as "theoretic form of the soul," represents that common ground between all persons, and as Henderson moves closer to Dahfu, by recognizing the lion, he comes to recognize that extra dimension in himself as well. "I think maybe my person is sacred," he says triumphantly (p. 234). He sees himself at a beginning, relating with perfect primacy: "It is very early in life, and I am out in the grass. The sun flames and swells; the heat it emits is its love, too. I have this selfsame vividness in my heart. There are dandelions. I try to gather up this green. I put my love-swollen cheek to the yellow of the dandelions. I try to enter into this green" (p. 238). Henderson marvels at the great "instrument of life." "Played wrong, why does it suffer so? Right, how can it achieve so much, reaching even God?" (p. 240).

But *Henderson the Rain King* is not the story only of Eugene Henderson. As a story of transcendentally mutual relationship, it is a story about Dahfu as well. The surprising turn of events at the novel's end allows Bellow to portray, better than ever before, one vital nature of relation as Hasidism defines it — namely, that it is self-regenerative, that it passes itself on, bringing new life, creation continuous. "Creation does not merely take place once in the beginning," Buber has said, "but also at every moment throughout the whole of time."[37] Malamud gets this said in *The Assistant* with much the same tone: Frank's conversion dance on the grave of the grocer at once resurrects Bober and Bober's son; a grocer dies and a new grocer puts on the apron.

Dahfu, we learn at one point in the story, is a "becoming" man himself. "The central process of movement," Frye says of the myth, "is that of the death and rebirth, or the disappearance and return, or the incarnation and withdrawal of a god."[38] According to the tradition of his tribe, when a king dies, his soul takes new shape, first in the form of a maggot, and then in the form of a lion cub. This lion cub is both the converted soul of the old king and the not fully converted soul of the new. He embodies the souls of two men in one form. After an interval, the new king is announced as the last conversion of the lion cub. It then becomes the new king's responsibility to capture the lion, which is still considered a theoretic form of his father's soul. Dahfu has not yet captured his father, whose soul now rests in a fully grown lion. At the story's end, Henderson and Dahfu go out to hunt the lion and in the process Dahfu is mortally wounded. As he dies, he explains to Henderson that he (Henderson) is the new King, since the Rain King, if there is no child of age, must succeed the old ruler. Imprisoned after Dahfu's death, Henderson notices a little lion cub tethered to a pole outside his cell. This cub will soon be presented as Dahfu's converted soul. After a time Henderson will then be presented as the next conversion of the lion cub, or Dahfu's soul. Hence this lion cub represents the perfect union of Henderson and Dahfu, each having left becoming for being. "It is a regular feature of all such myths," — Frye again — "that the dying god is reborn as the same person. Hence the mythical or abstract structural principle of the cycle is that the continuum of identity in the individual life from birth to death is extended from death to rebirth."[39] Buber explains Dahfu's sacrifice and salvation in giving up his life to a form of the soul: "And thirdly," Buber says, describing the three ways to reach the *Thou*, "there is pure effective action without arbitrary self-will. This is higher than the spirit of knowledge and the spirit of art, for here the mortal, bodily man . . . outlasts it as structure. . . . Here the *Thou* appeared to the man out of deeper mystery, addressed him even out of the darkness, and he responded with his life. This life may have fulfilled the law or broken it; both are continually necessary that spirit may not die on earth." [40] That spirit may not die on earth — Dahfu converts his life into a form of the soul, giving his soul to Henderson, to burst his spirit's sleep, that spirit may not die on earth. "This life is presented then," Buber continues, "to those who come later, to teach them not what is and must be, but how life is lived in the spirit, face to face with the *Thou*. That is, it is itself ready on every occasion to become *Thou* for them, and open up the world of *Thou*." [41]

Such is the true depth of Henderson's relationship with Dahfu. Escaping from his prison cell, he takes the lion cub — Dahfu, Dahfu's soul, his soul — and sets out for Danbury, Connecticut, his spirit awake, eager to meet his wife and children once again.

Henderson has found the rhythm of the living universe — "There's no getting away from it," he says finally (p. 276). So long a prodigal, he ends the journey and joins the family: "The grass should be my cousins" (p. 276). In tune, thus, with the mysterious symphony of life, Henderson rests in the state of *shiflut*, *hitlahabut*'s transformation, feeling, just as Buber describes it, "the universal generation as a sea, and oneself as a wave in it."

Giving his protagonist a form with which to resolve his quest, Bellow has done the same for himself, working within the frame of the myth — what Frye calls "the imitation of actions near or at the conceivable limits of desire." [42] But it is, in the end, a special kind of myth — a myth, first and last, about human relationship; a myth about human being above all, once again Hasidic in origin and intention: "I hold the myth to be indispensable," Buber writes, "yet I do not hold it to be central, but man and ever again man. Myth must authenticate itself in man and not man in myth." [43] Our special dimension cannot be proven in myth, so much as our self-recognition can prove what myth says about us to be true. In this way, amidst the unlikely backdrop of darkest Africa, in Henderson's need "to redeem the present and discover the future," Bellow's novel asks to leave becoming and genuinely be an authentic tale for twentieth-century America.

farbrengen

As we were about to separate I told Reuven I didn't think I could get myself up at four in the morning, especially to kill chickens. "Roosters," he said. "The women will kill chickens."

Reuven was my chaver, literally friend. We studied, as was the tradition, in pairs. One finds a chaver to be one's teacher and student of Talmud and Tanya (the mystical book of Lubavitcher Hasidism), after the rabbi's lessons. Mine taught me many other things besides: that the little ⓤand K on food packages were kashruth signs, standing for "Union of Orthodox Rabbis" and "Kosher" respectively; but that Ⓐstood for the American Can Company.On this day, only a few days from Yom Kippur, the Day of Atonement, he was telling me about the mitzvah of kaporis to be performed some minutes before sunrise tomorrow.

It can't be time when, later, Reuven rings the bell; I'm sure I've just fallen asleep. And it's dark out. And if I pretend I don't hear him then my wife will be awakened by the ringing. And certainly she won't go to the door, since her hair isn't covered and she knows Reuven will not enter a house with another man's wife if it is not established that the husband is both present and awake. And he's not. And it's still ringing.

"How do I get there?" this, from me, in the car, as I try the starter.

"I don't know exactly. They said to follow the cars."

It is a little after four in the morning and all the cars look as if they have been followed as far as one can. I say something to this effect and Reuven laughs. But he has been doing that since I opened the door. I had expected this early morning cheer to annoy me but it doesn't. Maybe because the cheer is so quiet.

"Why don't you go to the shul and we'll pick someone up," he says.

Five blocks later there is, sure enough, human activity, dozens of men dressed in long black coats, black hats, white muslin shirts, beards of various size and color. This is a standard procedure, standing in front of the shul ("school," synagogue) if you need a ride. For each of them the walk from home to shul is the closest, most familiar walk in the world. Aside from work, anything farther away, it seemed, would be an extension of the shul, and getting there only meant getting to the shul. Those with cars would be by to find those without.

The two that joined us didn't know exactly where we wanted to go either, but they knew the general direction and were similarly unconcerned. "We'll run into them."

This was true again. After a time on deserted Brooklyn streets there suddenly appeared a swarm of activity, cars parked in no order, blocking each other, left in the street. We were at a poultry butcher shop.

Inside there was a flurry of chicken feathers and black-suited men, Hasidic women wrestling down poultry cages or standing in pairs. We had come late, someone said to us, running past us, as if we had missed the better part of some bargain sale. It was not late enough for me. Almost from the moment I entered I felt I had found the experience that could only be experience; I was weak in my knees and nauseous in my stomach. I had had no breakfast and the smell was incredibly dense.

After the moment in which I thought I might faint
had passed, Reuven and I went to find our roosters.
It was a self-service affair. Grabbing one by its legs
and neck I could do no better at containing the bird
than the old Hasids who looked slightly frightened
and disgusted all around me. In this we were
completely alike: urban through and through.

Although I had learned the prayer — an especially difficult one, I found — it had not occurred to me
how different holding a rooster while reading from a
prayer book might be from, say, holding a cup of
wine or a loaf of bread. I stumbled through it, but I
think the message came across. Roughly translated:
I had many times failed myself during the year now
ending; I had taken such poor care of my life I could
not be sure I deserved to keep on living; but I could
change, I am made of promise; this rooster is now
for the moment me; it will die that I can go on living.

After the prayer I stood in a line feeling grateful to
the old bird, waiting to have the butcher, before my
eyes, cut its neck. To stand in a line with a group of
dignified, elaborately dressed men and women,
each holding a large, squirming bird, and trying, for
some reason, to look as if they were only waiting
together for a bus — that is why I was given breath
today, I thought, putting it in terms the Hasids used.

There were not many people behind us in line. We
had come late. When an old Hasid came in through
the door a dawn light came through with him. He
was in a very great hurry, turning over crates in
search of an unblessed bird. He found one and thrust
it before a butcher's assistant. "A zucher?" he said
wildly, asking if it were a male. It was not. "Oy" said
the old man, throwing it in the air, searching for another, checking the light outside. "A zucher? A
zucher?" I heard him say a second time. He was

panicked that the sun would rise before he had traded places with a bird.

I came home and went to sleep. When I awoke there were three pieces of mail in the mailbox.

A card from a fellow student at the yeshivah: "A man who did t'chuvah ["returned"] and closed his store on Saturdays is losing customers. It is our responsibility to help. Rosen's Laundry and Dry Cleaning. 342 Union Street."

A flyer from a Manhattan chapter of Esalen: "You are invited to a meeting which will be led by Dr. Jack Revere guiding some experiences involving the sharing of secrets among strangers."

A card from Norfolk and Dedham Mutual Fire Insurance Company: "In conjunction with your application for insurance, a routine inspection will be made developing information on your general reputation, character and mode of living."

THE BELLOW AND THE MELAMED: THE NOVEL AS EDUCATION

A story I heard often among the Lubavitcher Hasidim concerned the traveler in search of the palace. Not lost exactly — he knew after all where he *wanted* to go — he was only in need of instruction. For this he brought himself to the local rabbi; the word means teacher, no more. "There are two ways," the rabbi said, after hearing the man out. "A short way and a long way. And —" "But then tell me the short way," the traveler said, interrupting. At this the rabbi smiled. "There is no short way," he said. "There are two ways: a short way and a long way; and a long way and a short way." Now the traveler was quite confused. "Send me on the way that is shorter." "Neither way is shorter," the rabbi said. "Send me the way that is most simple." At this the rabbi smiled and said nothing at all. "Then just send me the first way," the traveler said, exasperated.

So the rabbi instructed the traveler along the short way and the long way. Very quickly he found himself breaking through the forest into a great clearing, where lying before him he saw plainly and completely the immense and glittering palace. Yet all around the palace there stood a tall fence, its posts too narrowly spaced for the traveler to squeeze through. There was no course other than to follow the fence around the palace, hoping to find an open gate. There where he wanted to be, but not there, the traveler walked for a great time and a great distance, never taking his eyes off the palace, which he could see clearly but could not enter. Many times he thought he would quit, thought there may be no gate at all, thought he could stand no longer the torment of seeing his goal so clearly — with each step! now from this angle, now from that — while being unable to attain it.

Sometime later, long after he had found the gate, entered through it, and returned to the village, the traveler had occasion again to go to the palace. He returned to the same village, to the same rabbi, and said, "No course could be so difficult as the one you set for me. Tell me please the other way." The rabbi smiled and gave directions for the long way and the short way, and the traveler set out. Again he was quickly in the forest, but this time there was no clearing. Only more forest. The traveler walked a great time and a great distance until the view behind was as unfamiliar and barren of signs of relief as the view ahead. Many times he thought he must quit, thought there might be no end to this dense travel, thought he could stand no longer the torment of moving without apparent progress, of having at each moment to conquer doubt even in the reality of the goal. Yet when he came, finally, at a time past hoping, to the clearing and the palace, he stood before the open gate.

"The principle of human life," Martin Buber writes in 'Distance and Relation, 'is not simple but two-fold, being built up in a two-fold movement which is of such kind that the one movement is the presupposition of the other."[1] Here he calls these movements "the primal setting at a distance," and "entering into relation." The long way and the short way do not oppose each other but define the movement of the spirit by their relationship to each other. Different routes to the palace are different not by being long or short, but by differently binding the long to the short. The novels that have been present to us are stories of the spirit's travel along its way, the education of the human soul. They are about the struggle to bind the one way to the other to complete a journey. For while the long way and the short way presuppose each other, their binding is not at all given but ever the work of raising the holy sparks. "With the appearance of the first [way]," Buber says, "nothing more than room for the second is given. It is only at this point that the real history of the spirit begins."[2]

But Bellow and Malamud, historians of human spirit, each

teach a separate way of going. Frank Alpine and Yakov Bok, prisoners of history, men who must serve time, find themselves treading the long way of *aboda* before they reach the opening of *hitlahabut*. (*"Hitlahabut* is as far from *aboda* as is fulfillment from longing, and yet it streams out of *aboda* as does the finding of God from the seeking."[3]) Augie March and Eugene Henderson — burners, kissers of life — are bound to quite another kind of education. In the presence throughout of a kind of mysteriousness to the everyday, they hunger to pierce through mere apprehension and *connect* ("I want! I want!"). Having completed the short way, burning for Zion, near without knowledge, it is their work to win through *hitlahabut* to learn of the limits that *permit* relation, called by the Hasidim *shiflut*. ("And yet the individual is not a whole but a part. And the purer and more perfect he is, so much the more intimately does he know that he is a part and so much the more actively there stirs in him the community of existence. That is the mystery of humility."[4])

"I don't believe in the untested spirit," Malamud said to me some years ago.[5] "Untested, one is unrevealed." The education of the long way before the short, of *aboda,* is a test — of faith and one's capacity to reach relation, of faith in the very reality of the goal itself. The journey is a stern one; it feels unrelenting; but it is surely not an exercise in pessimism, a mood other critics have attached to Malamud's work. "*The Assistant, The Fixer* — it's ridiculous to claim that these are pessimistic books," he said to me. Then he spoke of Alpine and Bok as if they had lives independent of their author, as, upon the books' completion, they no doubt do. "What strikes me about them," he said, "is that all throughout they have possibilities. They have opportunities to leave. They have a way out, but they never give up." It is this that makes their confinement *aboda,* service, the long way: that in large measure their confinement is built of their own choices, that this arduous journey of the spirit is a test they set for themselves. "My belief," Malamud said, "is in human possibility." The education of possibility is the work of *The Assistant* and *The Fixer*, a service whose goal is finally the mysterious. "This is my job," Malamud said, "the exemplification of mystery."

But the open space, the relief from "the narrow ridge" that Malamud's protagonists accomplish as graceful conclusion to the long way — this is where we find Augie at his story's beginning: "going at things free style," celebrating "*moha*, the opposition of the finite." Henderson, too, "had known these moments when the dumb begins to speak, when I hear the voices of objects and colors; then the physical universe starts to wrinkle and change and heave and rise and smooth, so it seems that even the dogs have to lean against a tree, shivering" (p. 87). Bellow's protagonists already hear the primary speech of the world, yet a long way must be part of their journey as well. They must work, not for the moment when they might hear the dumb begin to speak, but for the moment when they will be able to *answer* primary word with primary word.[6] They find themselves in that space that "make[s] your breast and bowel draw at various places from your trying to respond," according to Augie; it "make[s] you attempt to answer and want to stir" (p. 342). Their longing is different from that of *aboda*, but longing there is, there before the palace, faced but unfound; there, needing a distance in order to move closer to the goal. For underneath the crazy air and Chagall colors of their stories, nothing comes through so strongly about these two, Augie and Henderson, as their *earnestness*. "A pretty gay numero" or not, ecstatic or not, Augie's moves across inner and outer geography are finally a matter of search, as every picaro's must be; bountifully provided for, Henderson is profoundly hungry.

"Well, now," Augie says, blocked at the palace fence, ecstasy uneducated, "who can really expect the daily facts to go, toil or prisons to go, oatmeal and laundry tickets and all the rest, and insist that all moments be raised to the greatest importance, demand that everyone breathe the pointy, star-furnished air at its highest difficulty, abolish all brick, vault-like rooms, all dreariness and live like prophets or gods? Why everybody knows this triumphant life can only be periodic. So there's a schism about it, some saying only this triumphant life is real and others that only the daily facts are. For me there was no debate, and I made speed into the former" (p. 204). Here, early in his journey, Augie is all short way, all "triumphant life," by which he means all life apart from the daily dust; just as the assistant and the fixer, at their start, are all the long way, all "no God at all," all "death tomb positive." But what each learns is that the palace is entered neither by the long way nor the short, but by finding a relation between the two. Augie needs to learn that "the daily facts" do not expunge the "triumphant life," that the finite and the infinite do not drive each other out, but are to be brought together in relation, bound over each to the other, and that thereby the palace is won. For Augie and Henderson, then, oddly, the need is to marry the finite, to learn about limit, in order to reach the illimitable. "Every form of relation," Buber writes, "in which the spirit's service of life is realized has *its special objectivity, its structure of proportions and limits* which in no way resists the fervour of personal comprehension and penetrations."[7] Lacking this it is "feverish and unsteady."[8]

It is *hitlahabut* uneducated, unrelated to the daily facts, that appears to Bellow's Mr. Sammler the modern danger: "At the present level of crude vision agitated spirits fled from the oppressiveness of 'the common life,' separating themselves from the rest of their species, from the life of the species, hoping perhaps to get away (in some peculiar sense) from the death of the species."[9] "The reason why I didn't see things as they were," Augie says at the end, "was that I didn't want to; because I couldn't love them as they were. But the challenge was not to better them in your mind but to put every human weakness into the picture — the bad, the criminal, sick, envious, scavenging, wolfish, the living in the dying. Start with that" (p. 453). Ecstasy unbound to the "common life" is fever, madness; the fever of the holy sparks trapped within, the madness of the short way before the long. Such "madness is also masquerade," as old Sammler puts it, "the project of a deeper vision, a result of the despair we feel before infinities and eternities."[10] It is the despair brought on by wanting the infinity ("this ceaseless voice in my heart, 'I want! I want!'") as something apart from the dust of daily living; it is, as Buber says, that "wretchedness grounded in the resistance to the entrance of the holy into the lived life." This Augie learns at the end of his travels around the palace fence, where he, like "wisdom [has] had to spread and knot out in all directions" (p. 316): "Where striving stops there they are as a gift" (p. 472). The axial lines run through, not above, the oatmeal and the laundry tickets.

If Malamud's two protagonists are all "part," collecting themselves, coming into wholeness only at the end of the long way, Bellow's are all "whole," unable to see how they are also only a part. This is the kind of limit of which Henderson needs to learn in order to move closer to the palace. "The tendency of your conscious is to isolate self," the King, Dahfu, tells Henderson. "On earth sensitive ignorance still dreamed of being separate and 'whole,' " Sammler says, inveighing another time against the short way uncompleted. " 'Whole'? What 'whole'? A childish notion. It led to all this madness, mad religions, LSD, suicide, to crime."[11] The long way after the short, the stance of *shiflut*, has something to do with learning that "the individual is not a whole but a part. And the purer and more perfect he is, so much the more intimately does he know that he is a part and so much the more actively there stirs in him the community of existence." Dahfu educates Henderson to this mystery, forces him out of his isolation of self, by casting him into relation first with the lion, then with himself. But he does so not really as a *means* to the satisfaction of Henderson's demands as Henderson understands them — that he fulfill himself, burst his spirit's sleep, that he cease becoming for being — but because he, the King, sees *relation itself* as the *true* end of Henderson's ceaseless inner voice. Poor Henderson, victim of his times, must understand his own spirit's demand as amounting ultimately to a hunger for "personal growth," or the "actualization" of his "human potential"; it takes dark Africa, "older than Ur," to teach him that these are but the derivatives of accomplishing the actual demand; poor Henderson, casting as being itself what is more of becoming. "For the inmost growth of the self," Buber says, "is *not* accomplished, as people like to suppose today, in man's relation to himself, but in the relation between the one and the other, between men, that is, pre-eminently in the mutuality of the making present."[12] In "making present" I give up wholeness as the goal, give up the palace, and, giving it up, find it. "Where striving stops there [it is] as a gift."

In "making present" I give up wholeness ("Making present: . . . that event in which I experience, let us say, the specific pain of another in such a way that I feel what is specific in it, not, therefore a general discomfort or state of suffering, but this particular pain as the pain of the other. This making present increases until it is a paradox in the soul when I and the other are embraced by a common living situation, and, let us say, the pain which I inflict upon him surges up in myself, revealing the abyss of the contradictoriness of life between man and man."[13]); I give up wholeness as the goal, give up the palace I see before me, and, giving it up, find it

("At such a moment [this making present], something can come into being which cannot be built up in any other way"14). "Sent forth from the natural domain of species," Buber writes, concluding his essay "Distance and Relation," "into the hazard of the solitary category, surrounded by the air of a chaos which came into being with him, secretly and bashfully he watches for a Yes which allows him to be and which can come to him only from one human person to another. It is from one man to another that the heavenly bread of self-being is passed." 15 And now, that Yes is returned, the long way after the short completed. Striving throughout his story to answer the primary word he heard so often it had come to sound like a taunt, Henderson now "gave myself to it, and all my sorrow came out in the roaring. My lungs supplied the air but the note came from my soul" (p. 225).

A story Buber records: When Rabbi Yeheskel Landau came to Prague, he spoke to his congregation Sabbath after Sabbath of nothing else except the bitter need of the destitute in the city. One had expected to hear from his mouth profound meanings of interpretations and subtle meanings of disputations, but he only thought of reminding them of the wretched who spread out unrelieved, unnoticed, in this lane and its surroundings. "Help! Go there even today in the evening and help!" Thus he called ever again. But the people took it for a sermon and were vexed that it was so insipid and flat.

Then on a busy market day something wonderful took place. Right through the middle of the tumult came the rabbi and remained standing in the center of the thickest swarm as though he had wares to offer for sale and only waited for a favorable moment to commend them to the crowd. Those who recognized him passed the incomprehensible fact on to others; from everywhere traders and buyers crowded to that place; they stared at him, but no one dared to question him. Finally there broke from the lips of one who imagined himself intimate with him, "What is our rabbi doing here?"

At once Rabbi Yeheskel began:

"If a table has three legs and a piece is broken off of one of the three legs, what does one do? One supports the leg as well as one can, and the table stands. But now if still another of the three legs breaks in two, there is no longer a support. What does one do then? One shortens the third leg too, and the table stands again.

"Our sages say: 'The world stands on three things: on the teaching, on the service, and on the deeds of love.' When the holiness is destroyed, then the leg of service breaks. Then our sages support it by saying: 'Service with the heart, that is what is meant by prayer.' But now when the acts of love disappear and the second leg suffers injury, how shall the world still endure? Therefore, I have left the house of teaching and have come to the market place. We must shorten the leg of teaching in order that the table of the world may again stand firm."[16]

The novel as literary form is a kind of adoration of the particular; it is "stuck on" the concrete, the laundry lists, the oatmeal, the flies in Augie's barroom. It is articulate, built of article, pieces, flex; all for the purpose, like Henderson's lion, of forcing relation: "When she gives her tail a flex it strikes against my heart." In this the novel itself is Hasidic, but a novel about the travels of the spirit especially so. It teaches in the marketplace to balance the table of the world.

The world in the novels of Bellow and Malamud is a concrete world *pretending*; but this in the literal, Latin sense, a "holding forward" of the everyday. Behind, burst-ready, concealed: "something wonderful" about to take place. This is artifice, but whose? "From of old Israel has proclaimed that the world is not God's place, but that God is the place of the world," Buber writes.[17] And yet the concrete worlds Bellow and Malamud create — worlds of intense *readiness* — are, at each story's beginning, *only* ready; the sacred is not by itself bodying forth. For this there must be education — the literal sense again — a leading out. Here the novelists construct the concrete world as the Hasids do.

Hasidism expresses this principle [that God is the place of world] in a new way, namely in a practical way . . . [it] is not a purely objective statement, which remains true independently of the life lived by the individual; it is only when it is brought into actual contact with the individual that the world becomes sacramental. That is, in the actual contact of these things and beings with this individual, with you, with me. In all of these things and beings dwells the divine spark, and all of these things and beings are given to this particular individual that this particular individual may through his contact with them redeem the divine spark. Man's existence in the world becomes fraught with meaning, because the things and beings of the world have been given to him in their sacramental potentiality. [18]

Teaching us about "this particular individual" — Frank and Augie, Yakov and Eugene — living in a potentially sacramental world, Bellow and Malamud design anew the idea that the novel dwells in the particular to make its way to the universal.

Teachers of the spirit, which they know "is not given to us apart from man: all the spiritual life which is given to us has its reality in him,"[19] Bellow and Malamud, like Buber, like Rabbi Yeheskel in the marketplace, reject, by the vehicle of instruction they choose, any approach to the holy that bypasses the particular. They are, none of them, religionists: "The real communion of man with God has not only its place in the world, but also its object," says Buber.

God speaks to man in the things and beings whom he sends him in life. Man answers through his dealings with these things and beings. . . . But it is the ancient danger, perhaps it is the most extreme danger and temptation of man, that something comes to be taken away and isolated from the human side; what has been taken away then becomes independent, rounded off and completed till it looks as if it were interchangeable with the whole from which it sprang; and then it is substituted for the real communion. The *ur*-danger of man is "religion," . . . then [the forms] cease to embody the consecration of the lived, everyday life, and become instead the means of it . . . the "God" of this divine service is no longer God, it is the mask, the real partner of the communion is no longer there, the worshipper gesticulates into the empty air. [20]

The novel's adoration of the particular protects against the emptiness of the air within; if the novel, further, takes up ultimate concerns it insures an air suffused by Forster's "bar of light," the novelistic form, in Forster's terms, of "prophesy." In

Hasidic terms, it is the voice of Holy Insecurity, the essence of which is the "ever-anew" of each situation. Israel's prophets, Buber says, "always aimed to shatter all security and to proclaim in the opened abyss of the final insecurity the unwished for God who demands that His human creatures become real . . . the key to this 'holy insecurity' is the 'ever-anew' of each situation as opposed to the 'once for all' with which man tries to abstract himself from the concrete." [21] The key is in the "ever-anew," that is to say, the novel.

"In a town not far from that in which Rabbi Nachum of Tschernobil lived, some of his disciples were once sitting at 'the farewell of the Queen,' which once more gathers the devout together before the Sabbath is ushered out; and as they were sitting, they spoke of the account which the soul has to give of itself in its deepest self-reflection. Then it came over them in their fear and humility that it seemed to them as if the life of them all were thrown away and squandered, and they said to each other that there would be no hope for them any more were it not that it comforted them and gave them confidence that they were allowed to join themselves to the great *zaddik*, Rabbi Nachum. Then they all rose, driven by a common desire, and set forth on the way to Tschernobil. At the same time as this was happening, Rabbi Nachum was sitting in his house, giving account of his soul. Then it seemed also to him in his fear and humility as if his life were thrown away and squandered, and that all his confidence came from only this one thing, that these God-drunken men had joined themselves to him. He went to the door, and looked towards the dwelling-place of the disciples; and when he had been standing there for a time, he saw them coming. 'In this moment,' added the *zaddik*, when he told of the event, 'did the ring snap fast.' " [22]

The characters of Bellow and Malamud have to *work upon* the world to make it yield its holy sparks, to release their own. Nothing is given without relation, but it is just as important to see that the education the books are about is a mutual one, a leading out from both sides, the world, as creation, itself in continuous need of redemption.

For there is another education, again mutual: not only the characters, but the artists themselves, do work upon the world, redemption through what Malamud calls "exemplification" when he defines his work as "the exemplification of mystery."[23] Their art is itself both the form and the symbol of this mutual leading out. "It is, indeed," Buber writes, "neither the mystery of the things nor that of the spirit that is represented in art, but the relation between the two."[24] "Art is neither the impression of natural objectivity nor the expression of spiritual subjectivity," he says, "but it is the work and witness of the relation between the *substantia humana* and the *substantia rerum*, it is the realm of 'the between' which has become form."[25] Henderson in the jungle is like the artist, the one who has "got to go on because I haven't reached that depth yet," that depth he cannot reach until he has found a form, that form lacking which he is the "mystic without vehicle." Once the foe of all measure, Henderson learns what the novelists know, that "this is not a sick and hasty ride, helpless, through a dream into oblivion. No, sir! It can be arrested by a thing or two. By art, for example. The speed is checked, the time is redivided. Measure! That great thought. Mystery!" (p. 149) This is Buber's "special objectivity," that "structure of proportion and limit" that is as necessary a feature of ultimate relation as "the fervour of personal comprehension and penetration." The novelist redeems creation by giving "the soul as form," in Buber's words, "such great power over the soul as matter" that "chaos is subdued, and shaped into cosmos."[26]

But this brings us to yet a third education: for the novel as form is redemption *become creation*, a teacher itself in need of redemption. This continual transformation Malamud himself seems to suggest when he says, of his "redeeming," extending his remark of a moment ago, that "exemplification of mystery is the *creation* of mystery." The artist's own saying of the primary word becomes itself a creation in the world, its spark entrapped, in danger of becoming "independent, rounded off and completed." The artist's *Thou* passes into an *It*, the New Criticism's separation of artist and completed artwork become Buber's "exalted melancholy of our fate." Having been in his way *responsible*, the artist now stands helpless, *as artist*, before his redemption become creation, his *Thou* passed over into *It*. The work, finished *by the author*, is "a thing among things," Buber says, "able to be experienced and described as a sum of qualities. *But from time to time it can face the receptive beholder in its whole embodied form.*" [27] Art's purpose, long defined — to delight and instruct — can be seen more reciprocally; for in being delighted and instructed, the reader — and only the reader — may at any moment move beyond (now redundant) "vicarious *experiencing*," and bring the work to burning again.

The story of the Hebrews' liberation, told at the Passover seder, cannot begin until the youngest among the company notices that things look strange at the table and asks for some instruction. The Lubavitcher Hasidim actively seek a stranger in the synagogue on Friday night to invite to their home for the Sabbath dinner. Made comfortable, the stranger, too, may eventually ask, "Why do you cover the bread before you bless the wine?" and "What do you make of this week's Torah portion?" Certainly the child or the stranger have real needs; and the one who teaches may genuinely know of things or ways the child or stranger does not. But the relationship is not one-way. The teachers have their own needs. Without the question there will not be an answer. Without an answer the teacher ceases rediscovering what he or she believes *to be* the answer, ceases rediscovering what he or she believes, *Thou* passed over to *It*, unredeemed without new relation, a communion with empty air. We have need of the novel but the need is mutual. The novel, like Rabbi Nachum, is a teacher itself in need. The novel is not finished. Made with the fingers, it is *handed* to us, to mold and shape, to continue fashioning, re-creating in *the between*.

When the great Rabbi Israel Ba'al Shem Tov saw misfortune threatening the Jews, it was his custom to go into a certain part of forest to meditate. There he would light a fire, say a special prayer, and the miracle would be accomplished and the misfortune averted.

Later when his disciple, the celebrated Maggid of Mezritch, had occasion, for the same reason, to intercede with heaven, he would go to the same place in the forest and say: "Master of the Universe, listen! We do not know how to light the fire, but we are still able to say the prayer." And again the miracle would be accomplished.

Still later, Rabbi Moshe-Leib of Sasov, in order to save his people once more, would go into the forest and say: "We can no longer light the fire, nor do we know the secret meditations belonging to the prayer, but we do know the place in the forest to which it belongs — and that must be sufficient." And it was sufficient.

Then it fell to Rabbi Israel of Rizhyn to overcome misfortune. Sitting in his armchair, his head in his hands, he spoke to God: "We cannot light the fire, we cannot speak the prayers, and we do not know the place. All we can do is tell the story of how it was done, and this must be sufficient." And it was so. [28]

"The story is not ended," Gershom Scholem says. "It has not yet become history, and the secret life it holds can break out tomorrow in you or in me. Under what aspects this invisible stream of Jewish mysticism will again come to the surface we cannot tell." [29] Nor can I. Still — to bring this book-long suspicion to a close — I remember the words the Lubavitchers add when they finish the tale I have just told you: God made man, they say, because He loves stories.

NOTES

The works by Martin Buber are abbreviated in the notes in the following fashion:

Martin Buber, *A Believing Humanism: Gleanings,* Maurice Friedman, trans. (New York: Simon & Schuster, 1967). [Abbreviated: *Believing*]

_____, *Between Man and Man,* Ronald Gregor Smith, trans. (New York: Macmillan, 1965). [*Between*]

_____, *Eclipse of God: Studies in the Relation Between Religion and Philosophy* (New York: Harper & Brothers, 1952). [*Eclipse*]

_____, *Good and Evil* (New York: Scribner's, 1953). [*Evil*]

_____, *Hasidism* (New York: Philosophical Library, 1948). [*Hasidism*]

_____, *Hasidism and the Modern Man,* Maurice Friedman, trans. (New York: Horizon Press, 1958). [*Modern*]

_____, *I and Thou,* Ronald Gregor Smith, trans. (New York: Scribner's, 1958). [*Thou*]

_____, *Jewish Mysticism,* Lucy Cohen, trans. (London: J. M. Dent & Sons Ltd., 1931). [*Mysticism*]

_____, *The Knowledge of Man,* Maurice Friedman and Ronald Gregor Smith, trans. (New York: Harper & Row, 1965). [*Knowledge*]

_____, *The Legend of the Ba'al Shem Tov,* Maurice Friedman, trans. (New York: Harper & Brothers 1955). [*Legend*]

————, *Mamre: Essays in Religion*, Greta Hort, trans. (Melbourne: Melbourne University Press, 1946). [*Mamre*]

————, *The Origin and Meaning of Hasidism*, Maurice Friedman, trans. (New York: Horizon Press, 1960). [*Origin*]

————, *Tales of the Hasidim* (New York: Schocken Books, 1966). [*Tales*]

————, *Ten Rungs*, Olga Marx, trans. (New York: Schocken Books, 1947). [*Rungs*]

SH'MA YISRAEL
THE VOX CLAMANTIS

1. Djuna Barnes, *Nightwood* (New York: New Directions, 1937), p. 31.
2. D. H. Lawrence, *Studies in Classic American Literature* (New York: Viking Press, 1961), p. 7.
3. Saul Bellow, *Seize the Day* (New York: Viking Press, 1956), p. 76.
4. Though, oddly, he seems to have taken no notice of the uniqueness of this phenomenon, Buber joins me in this perception:". . . Hasidism had no impulse to tear out any part of the structure of traditional Law . . ." (Buber, *Mamre*, p. 78); ". . . thus without changing an iota of the old Law, the ritual, or the tradition of daily life, what had become old can live again in a new light and expression . . ." (Buber, *Mysticism*, p. xv).
5. Dorothy Van Ghent, *The English Novel — Form and Function* (New York: Harper & Row, 1953), p. 263.
6. The following discussion of the vertical and horizontal owes much to William Barrett's fine essay "The Testimony of Modern Art" in his book *Irrational Man* (New York: Doubleday, 1958).
7. Quoted by Barrett, ibid., p. 243.
8. Eric and Mary Josephson, "Introduction," *Man Alone,* Eric and Mary Josephson, eds. (New York: Dell, 1962), p. 44.
9. William Faulkner, *The Sound and the Fury* (New York: Scribner's, 1956). Future references appear internally.

10. These are the words of Marcus Klein, an accommodationist critic. See Marcus Klein, *After Alienation* (New York: World, 1964), p. 296.

11. Albert Camus, *The Myth of Sisyphus and Other Essays* (New York: Vintage, 1955), p. 91.

12. Klein, op. cit., p. 32.

13. The way novelists use their characters' sexuality can be seen in terms of these three underlying visions I am advancing here. While I do not mean to suggest that homosexuality is itself necessarily reflective of an accommodationist vision, it does seem that homosexuality is being appropriated by Baldwin — in *Giovanni's Room,* for example — as a powerful accommodationist image. This might be contrasted with the alienated image Hemingway achieves, or, on the other hand, the affirmative image Bellow achieves, out of the sexualities of Jake Barnes or Augie March.

14. James Gould Cozzens, *The Guard of Honor* (New York: Harcourt, Brace, & World, 1948). Future references appear internally.

15. Allen Ginsberg, *Kaddish and Other Poems* (San Francisco: City Lights, 1967).

16. Buber, *Modern,* p. 39.

17. Ibid., pp. 38 - 39.

18. Harvey Cox, *The Secular City* (New York: Macmillan, 1965), p. 16.

19. Barrett, op. cit., p. 78.

20. Ibid.

21. Ibid., pp. 35 - 36.

22. Buber, *Origin,* p. 27.

23. Buber, *Modern,* p. 49.

24. Ibid., pp. 32 - 33.

25. Buber, *Mamre,* p. 78.

26. Buber, *Modern,* p. 29, p. 31.

27. Buber, *Mamre,* pp. 105 - 106.

28. Buber, *Modern,* p. 31.

29. Buber, *Thou,* p. 115. Italics mine.

30. Buber, *Modern,* p. 43.

31. Buber, *Mamre,* pp. 106 - 107.

32. Buber, *Mysticism,* p. xv.

33. Ibid., p. xii.

34. Ibid., p. 1.

35. *"Hitlahabut* can appear in all places and at all times," says Buber (*Mysticism*, p. 1.). Says Augie March: "I was lying on the couch here before and [the axial lines] suddenly went quivering right straight through me." "The man of ecstasy would marvel and awaken and be aflame," says Buber (*Mysticism*, p. 2.) Says Augie: "Truth, love, peace, bounty, usefulness, harmony. And all noises and grates, distortion, chatter, distraction, effort, superfluity, passed off like something unreal." The man of ecstasy "marvels at the renewal of creation, at all times and in every moment," says Buber (*Mysticism*, p. 2). Says Augie: "At any time life can come together again and be regenerated." " 'Sweet suffering, I receive you in love,' " Buber tells us a dying *zaddik* said (*Mysticism*, p. 2). Says Augie: "Even his pains [the man attuned to the axial lines] will be joy if they are true. . . . Death will not be terrible to him if life is not."

36. Buber, *Mysticism,* p. 1.

37. Ibid., p. 9.

38. Ibid.

39. Ibid., p. 10.

40. Frank Alpine, as Helen quickly understands, has fragmented identity: ". . . something about him, evasive, hidden. He sometimes appeared to be more than he was, sometimes less. His aspirations were apart from the self he presented normally . . . there was more to him than his appearance. . . . You looked into mirrors and saw mirrors." Yakov Bok has the boatman transport him across the river, steps into Hell, and is immediately fragmented: He is Bok and Dologushev, of Yiddish tongue and Russian tongue, of Old Testament and New, married and unmarried. *The Assistant* and *The Fixer* are novels of *aboda*, of men collecting themselves, of movement toward atone- ·ment. Yakov and Alpine are, first, no Jews at all ("Stay a Jew, Yakov; don't give up our God." "I don't want either.") ("a stranger's presence below, a goy after all . . ."): then they are Jews in part ("He's half a Jew himself.") ("The Jew lay white and motionless on the couch. Frank gently removed his apron. Draping the loop over his own head, he tied the tapes around him."): and, finally, they are identified by the very Jews with whom they grew ("The Jews of Plossky District . . . shouted his name.") ("As Ida and Helen toiled up the stairs they heard the dull cling of

the register in the store and knew the grocer was the one
who had danced on the grocer's coffin.").

41. Buber, *Mysticism,* p. 19.
42. Bernard Malamud, *The Assistant* (New York: Signet Books, 1957), p. 151.
43. Ibid., p. 145.
44. Bernard Malamud, *The Fixer* (New York: Dell, 1966), p. 89.
45. Saul Bellow, *The Adventures of Augie March* (New York: Crest, 1965).
46. Saul Bellow, *Henderson the Rain King* (New York: Crest, 1958).
47. Saul Bellow, *Herzog* (New York: Viking, 1961), p. 8.
48. Buber, *Modern,* p. 115.
49. Buber, *Mysticism*, p. 30.
50. Buber, *Modern*, p. 26.
51. Buber, *Tales*, p. 267.
52. Ibid., p. 191.
53. Ibid., p. 254.
54. Ibid., p. 289.
55. Ibid., p. 212.
56. Buber, *Modern,* p. 24.
57. For an examination of just how indebted Buber is to the Bible for the formulation of his *I-Thou* philosophy and the shaping of neo-Hasidism, see Roy Oliver, *The Wanderer and the Way: The Hebrew Tradition in the Writings of Martin Buber* (Ithaca: Cornell University Press, 1968).
58. Buber, *Eclipse,* p. 66.
59. Quoted by Buber, ibid., p. 67.
60. Ibid., pp. 67 - 68.
61. Ibid., p. 69.
62. Buber, *Thou,* p. 5.
63. Ibid., p. 4.
64. Ibid., p. 6.
65. Ibid., p. 37.
66. Ibid., p. 38.
67. Ibid., p. 34.
68. Ibld., p. 8.
69. Bellow, *Augie March,* op. cit., p. 458.
70. Quoted in *Man Alone*, op. cit., p. 36.
71. Quoted in *Man Alone,* op. cit., p. 27.
72. Allen Ginsberg, *Kaddish and Other Poems,* op. cit.
73. Buber, *Modern*, p. 33.

74. Ibid., p. 35.
75. Cf. Malcolm L. Diamond, *Martin Buber* (New York: Oxford University Press, 1960), p. 35.
76. e. e. cummings, *Six Nonlectures* (New York: Atheneum, 1963), p. 7.
77. Keith Michael Opdahl, *The Novels of Saul Bellow* (University Park: Pennsylvania State University Press, 1967), p. 25.
78. Chester Eisenger, *Fiction of the Forties* (Chicago: University of Chicago Press, 1963), p. 344.
79. Barrett, op. cit., p. 58.
80. D. H. Lawrence, *The Rainbow* (New York: Modern Library, 1943), p. 2.
81. Buber, *Mysticism,* p. 5.
82. Buber, *Thou,* p. 34. Repetition mine.
83. My understanding and rendering of this vocabulary owe a great debt to the notes and words of Professor Peter Bien of Dartmouth College.
84. Buber, *Origin,* p. 199.
85. Opdahl, op. cit., p. 4.
86. Sidney Richman, *Malamud* (New York: Twayne Publishers, 1966), p. 77.
87. Malamud, *The Assistant,* op. cit., p. 14.
88. Bellow, *Henderson,* op. cit., p. 213.
89. Klein, op. cit., pp. 295 - 296.
90. Ibid., p. 296.
91. Ibid., p. 296.
92. Bellow, *Henderson,* op. cit., pp. 127 - 128.

THE ASSISTANT'S *SERVICE*

1. Joseph Conrad, "The Secret Sharer," in *The Portable Conrad* (New York: Viking Press, 1947), p. 658.
2. Djuna Barnes, *Nightwood,* (New York: New Directions, 1937), p. 3.
3. Yevgeny Yevtushenko, *Yevtushenko Poems,* Herbert Marshall, trans. (New York: E. P. Dutton, 1966). p. 105.
4. Buber, *Mysticism,* p. 10.
5. Buber, *Modern,* p. 78.

6. Bernard Malamud, *The Assistant* (New York: New American Library, 1957), p. 53. Future references appear internally.
7. Buber, *Mysticism,* p. 9.
8. Ibid.
9. Personal conversation, Cambridge, Massachusetts, April 23, 1968. For more of this conversation see the final chapter of the present work.
10. Buber, *Modern,* p. 94.
11. Buber, *Tales,* pp. 185 - 186.
12. Buber, *Mysticism,* p. 10.
13. Buber, *Modern,* pp. 98 - 99.
14. Ibid., pp. 104 - 105.
15. Buber, *Mysticism,* p. 9.
16. Buber, *Modern,* p. 86.
17. Ibid.
18. Ibid., p. 94.
19. Buber, *Mysticism,* p. 4.
20. Buber, *Modern,* p. 94.
21. Buber, *Thou,* p. 15.
22. Ibid., p. 67.

SERVING TIME: THE FIXER

1. Buber, *Thou,* p. 15.
2. Malcolm L. Diamond, *Martin Buber, Jewish Existentialist* (New York: Oxford University Press, 1960), p. 93.
3. Ruth Landes and Mark Zborowski, "Hypotheses Concerning the Eastern European Jewish Family," in *The Psychodynamics of American Jewish Life* (New York: Twayne Publishers, 1967), p. 24.
4. Bernard Malamud, *The Fixer* (New York: Dell, 1966), p. 14. Future references appear internally.
5. Quoted by Howard Morley Sachar, *The Course of Modern Jewish History* (New York: World Publishing, 1958).
6. In a *New York Times* article reporting on the Lubavitcher Hasidism's attempt to induce Jews in Central Park to tie on the phylacteries (*tefillin*), Rabbi Samuel Schrage is quoted:

" 'Young men, especially Jewish young men, are searching for mystic experiences like LSD, and pot, and gurus and mahareshis. We can give them mysticism.' A part of that mysticism, Rabbi Schrage said, is the belief that the tefillin, and the prayers that accompany the wearing of them, have enormous power to undo the enemies of Israel . . ." (Bernard Collier, "Hasidic Jews Confront Hippies to Press a Joyous Mysticism," *The New York Times,* May 27, 1968, p. 49.)

7. Montague D. Eder, "The Jewish Phylacteries and Other Jewish Ritual Observances," in *The Psychodynamics of American Jewish Life,* op. cit., p. 33.

8. Buber, *Thou,* p. 94.

9. Bernard Malamud, *The Natural* (New York: Dell, 1952), p. 33.

10. Ibid., p. 94.

11. Bernard Malamud, *A New Life* (New York: Dell, 1957), p. 80.

12. Ibid., p. 79.

13. Ibid., p. 182.

14. Buber, *Tales,* p. 275.

15. Frederic A. Doppell and David Polish, *A Guide for Reform Jews* (New York: Jenny Loundy Memorial Fund, 1957), p. 34.

16. Ibid., p. 37.

17. Buber, *Origin,* p. 50.

18. Doppell and Polish, op. cit., p. 39.

19. Buber, *Thou, p.* 70.

20. Ibid., p. 70.

21. Ibid.

22. Ibid., pp. 71 - 72.

23. Ibid.

24. Ibid., p. 72.

25. Ibid., p. 93.

26. Ibid., p. 72.

27. Ibid., p. 12.

28. Montague D. Eder, op. cit., p. 335.

29. Quoted by Diamond, op. cit., p. 94.

30. Buber, *Thou,* pp. 67 - 68.

31. Ibid., p. 76.

32. Geza Roheim, "Some Aspects of Semitic Monotheism," in *Psychoanalysis and the Social Sciences,* Vol. 4, Warner Muensterberger, ed. (New York: International Universities Press, 1955), p. 169.

THE ECSTASY
OF AUGIE MARCH

1. Norman O. Brown, *Love's Body* (New York: Random House, 1966), p. 40.
2. Buber, *Mysticism,* p. 2.
3. Ibid., p. 35.
4. Saul Bellow, *The Adventures of Augie March* (New York: Crest, 1955), p. 457. All future references appear internally.
5. Buber, *Mysticism,* p. 2. Emphasis mine.
6. Buber, *Modern,* p. 50.
7. M. H. Abrams, *A Glossary of Literary Terms* (New York: Holt, Rinehart & Winston, 1965), p. 59.
8. Buber, *Thou,* pp. 39 - 41.
9. Buber, *Origin,* p. 13.
10. Ibid., p. 106.
11. Buber, *Thou,* pp. 81 - 82.
12. Buber, *Modern,* p. 31.
13. Buber, *Thou,* p. 43.
14. Buber, *Origin,* p. 13.
15. Buber, *Legend,* p. 47.
16. See Marcus Klein, *After Alienation* (New York: World Publishing, 1964). See also the first chapter of the present book.
17. Buber, *Thou,* p. 75.
18. Buber, *Mysticism,* p. 7.
19. Ibid.
20. Ibid., p. 5.
21. Buber, *Thou,* pp. 87 - 88.
22. Ibid., p. 18, p. 39.
23. Ibid., p. 97.
24. Buber, *Mysticism,* p. 9.
25. Buber, *Thou,* p. 59.
26. Ibid., pp. 16 - 17.
27. Buber, *Modern,* p. 172.
28. Buber, *Thou,* p. 98.
29. Buber, *Modern,* p. 172.
30. Buber, *Thou,* p. 101.
31. Cf. Keith Michael Opdahl, *The Novels of Saul Bellow* (University Park: Pennsylvania State University Press, 1967).

32. Buber, *Modern,* p. 31.
33. Ibid., p. 36.
34. Ibid.
35. Ibid., p. 190.
36. Buber, *Thou,* p. 11.
37. Ibid., p. 82.
38. Buber, *Thou,* p. 39.
39. Ibid., p. 109.
40. Buber, *Modern,* pp. 110 - 111.
41. Ibid.
42. Ibid., pp. 172 - 173.
43. Buber, *Thou,* p. 59.
44. Buber, *Mysticism,* p. 5.
45. Chester E. Eisenger, *Fiction of the Forties* (Chicago: University of Chicago Press, 1963), p. 343.
46. Ibid.
47. Harvey Cox, *The Secular City* (New York: Macmillan, 1965), p. 2.
48. Opdahl, op. cit.
49. Buber, *Thou,* p. 10.
50. Buber, *Modern,* p. 43.
51. Buber, *Origin,* p. 106.
52. Buber, *Thou,* p. 111.

HENDERSON THE RAIN KING: A FORM TO BURST THE SPIRIT'S SLEEP

1. Walt Whitman, "The Mystic Trumpeter," in *The Portable Walt Whitman,* Mark Van Doren, ed. (New York: Viking Press, 1966), p. 16.
2. Quoted by Ralph Waldo Emerson in "The Poet," in *Emerson's Essays,* Irwin Edman, ed. (New York: Thomas Y. Crowell, 1951), p. 269.
3. Nikos Kazantzakis, *Report to Greco,* P. A. Bien, trans. (New York: Simon & Schuster, 1965), p. 16.

4. Buber, *Thou,* p. 39.
5. Ibid., p. 41.
6. Ibid., pp. 41 - 42.
7. Saul Bellow, *Henderson the Rain King* (New York: Fawcett Crest, 1965), p. 91. All future references appear internally.
8. Buber, *Legend,* p.xx.
9. Buber, *Evil,* p. 116.
10. Buber, *Legend,* p. xxi.
11. R. P. Blackmur, "Anna Karenina: The Dialectics of Incarnation," in *Kenyon Review,* XVII (1955), p. 433. See also Richard Foster, *The New Romantics* (Bloomington: Indiana University Press, 1962), p. 102, whose excellent chapter on Blackmur first directed me to the original article.
12. Blackmur, op. cit., p. 433.
13. Ibid.
14. Ibid., p. 440.
15. Buber, *Evil,* p. 127.
16. Northrup Frye, *Anatomy of Critism* (New York: Atheneum, 1967), p. 136.
17. Buber, *Origin,* p. 54.
18. Ibid.
19. Buber, *Modern,* p. 142.
20. Ibid.
21. Buber, *Origin,* p. 55.
22. Buber, *Thou,* p. 40.
23. Ibid., p. 109.
24. See the last few pages of "The Ecstasy of Augie March," in the present volume.
25. Buber, *Thou,* p. 41.
26. Buber, *Origin,* p. 106.
27. Buber, *Thou,* p. 82.
28. Frye, op. cit., p. 136.
29. Buber, *Modern,* p. 99.
30. There is a lovely example here (p. 146), of Henderson's outrageous voice: " 'Ha, ha!' I laughed and cried. 'Say, King! What's that? Oh, Jesus — come again? The pumps of firmament? Isn't that the dandiest!' "
31. Buber, *Evil,* p. 120.
32. Ibid.
33. Ibid., p. 129.
34. In "The Poet," op. cit., Emerson cites these lines from "the wise Spenser":

So every spirit, as it is most pure
And hath in it the more of heavenly light,
So it the fairer body doth procure
To habit it, and it more fairly dight,
With cheerful grace and amiable sight.
For, of the soul, the body form doth take,
For soul is form, and doth the body make.

35. Buber, *Thou,* p. 12.
36. Buber, *Evil,* p. 129.
37. Buber, *Origin,* p. 106.
38. Frye, op. cit., p. 158.
39. Ibid., p. 159.
40. Buber, *Thou,* p. 42.
41. Ibid.
42. Frye, op. cit., p. 136.
43. Buber, *Origin,* pp. 248 - 249.

THE BELLOW
AND THE MELAMED:
THE NOVEL AS EDUCATION

1. Buber, *Knowledge,* p. 60
2. Ibid., p. 64.
3. Buber, *Legend,* p. 24.
4. Ibid., pp. 42 - 43.
5. Personal conversation, Cambridge, Massachusetts, April 23, 1968. Further remarks by Malamud refer to this conversation.
6. No superiority is intended here. The routes to the palace are different (as suddenness differs from immediacy) but it is not a difference of betterness or sequentiality. *Hitlahabut* flowers from *aboda;* from *hitlahabut, shiflut.* But this is a circle not a hierarchy. From *shiflut, aboda:* Henderson returning to Danbury to love his family; yes — and why not? — to apply to medical school.
7. Buber, *Between,* p. 94. Emphasis mine.

8. Ibid.
9. Saul Bellow, *Mr. Sammler's Planet* (Greenwich: Fawcett Crest, 1969), p. 136.
10. Ibid.
11. Ibid., p. 166.
12. Buber, *Knowledge*, p. 71. Emphasis mine.
13. Ibid., p. 70.
14. Ibid.
15. Ibid., p. 71.
16. Buber, *Believing*, pp. 96 - 97.
17. Buber, *Mamre*, p. 105.
18. Ibid., pp. 105 - 106.
19. Buber, *Knowledge*, p. 59.
20. Buber, *Mamre*, p. 103.
21. Buber, *Origin*, p. 13.
22. Buber, *Mamre*, p. 96.
23. Personal conversation. See note 5.
24. Buber, *Knowledge*, p. 165.
25. Ibid., p. 66.
26. Buber, *Evil*, p. 129.
27. Buber, *Thou*, p. 10.
28. A synthesis drawn from the versions of Elie Wiesel, *The Gates of the Forest*, Frances Frenay, trans. (New York: Holt & Winston, 1966) and Gershom Scholem, *Major Trends in Jewish Mysticism* (Jerusalem: Schocken, 1941).
29. Scholem, op. cit., p. 350.

GLOSSARY

Aboda (Hebrew) literally, "work, service, devotion"; one of four interrelated dimensions of Hasidic spirit; see definition in text, pp. 21-22.

Ba'al Shem Tov (Hebrew) literally, "the Master of the Good Name"; title of affection and respect given to Israel ben Eliezer, mid-eighteenth-century healer and magic man whose ecstatic personality and vision of a secular spirituality drew people into what became the Hasidic community.

Bayith (Hebrew) literally, "homes"; *tefillin* boxes; see *Tefillin*.

B'nai B'rith (Hebrew) literally, "the Children of the Covenant"; the Jewish people.

Chaver (Hebrew) literally, "friend"; partner in study.

Farbrengen (Yiddish) literally, "gathering," or "recreational gathering"; the gathering of the Hasidic community around the *rebbe* for story and song, especially on the afternoon of the Sabbath; see definition in text, p. 35.

Hasid (Hebrew) literally, "pious one"; name given derisively by orthodox adversaries to followers of, and upon, the Ba'al Shem Tov.

Hasidism a popular mystical Jewish movement arising in mid-eighteenth-century Poland-Lithuania, distinguished by cohesive communal living, antiasceticism, a sense of the immanence of the divine, a dialectical — rather than dichotomous — relationship between matter and spirit, ecstasy, music, and charismatic leadership.

Hitlahabut (Hebrew) literally, "ecstasy, burning enthusiasm"; one of four interrelated dimensions of Hasidic spirit; see definition in text, pp. 21-22.

Kaporis (Hebrew) literally, "fowls"; pre-Yom Kippur ritual in which one's sins are symbolically transferred to a fowl of one's own sex; the fowl is sacrificed and donated to charity.

Kashruth (Hebrew, from *kosher*) the laws pertaining to diet; what is fit to eat, how it should be prepared, how it should be consumed; for example, some animals, birds, and fish may be eaten and others may not; animals are to be slaughtered humanely; meat and milk are not to be consumed in the same meal.

Kavana (Hebrew) literally, "directed intention"; rabbinically, the state of concentration in prayer, or purposefulness in the carrying out of the commandments (*mitzvahs*); one of four interrelated dimensions of Hasidic spirit; see definition in text, pp. 21-22.

Kosher (Hebrew) literally, "fitting, proper."

Kreplach (Yiddish) boiled dumpling stuffed with meat.

Lubavitch Hasidism Hasidic sect founded by Schneur Zalman in the small Russian town of Lubavitch in early 1800s, now an international community centered in the United States; distinguished from other Hasidic sects by its openness and outreach, and by its integration of the intellectual and theoretic into the ecstatic "hallowing of the everyday."

Maggid (Hebrew) literally, "one who relates"; a popular, usually wandering teacher and preacher; spiritually, one who reveals the secrets of God.

Matzoh (Hebrew) literally, "unleavened bread," prepared carefully and elaborately to avoid the possibility of fermentation of the flour; the only bread that may be eaten during Passover, it commemorates the speedy exit from Egypt when the Jews could not wait for the dough to rise.

Mazel (Hebrew) literally, "luck, fortune."

Melamed (Hebrew) a teacher.

Mikvah (Hebrew) literally, "a collection [of water]"; ritual bath.

Mitzvah (Hebrew) literally, "commandment, duty"; colloquially, "good deed."

Neo-Hasidism twentieth-century theological and philosophical appropriation of Hasidism, most notably by Martin Buber, Abraham Heschel, and Isaac Leib Peretz.

Passover (in Hebrew, *Pesach*) spring festival commemorating the Exodus from Egypt.

Rebbe (Hebrew acronym formed from "Rosh B'nai Yisroel," "head of the children of Israel") title of affection and respect given by Hasidim to their leader, who is a combination of exegetical scholar, spiritual guide, psychotherapist, political leader, storyteller, and mystic in the material world.

Shiflut (Hebrew) literally, "humility"; one of four interrelated dimensions of Hasidic spirit; see definition in text, pp. 21-22.

Sh'ma Yisroel (Hebrew) literally, "Hear O Israel"; first words of the most fundamental prayer in the Hebrew liturgy.

Shtetl (Yiddish) literally, "little village"; small, intimate communities in Eastern Europe where many Jews lived from the sixteenth to nineteenth centuries.

Shul (Yiddish) literally "school"; the synagogue, which in Hasidic communities is a place of learning and socializing as well as worship.

Talmud (Hebrew) literally, "study, learning"; the written commentaries and interpretations; the *Mishnah* and *Gemara*.

Tchuvah (Hebrew) literally, "return"; penance, a return to the commandments.

Tefillin (Hebrew) phylacteries; two small boxes containing passages from Scripture that are fastened, with leather strips, to the hand and head in morning prayer; "thou shalt bind them for a sign upon thy hand and a frontlet between thine eyes"; a literal "tying in" to an ancient spiritual history.

Yeshivah (Hebrew) a school for Talmudic learning.

Yihud (Hebrew) literally, "unity"; theologically, the unity of the transcendent.

Yom Kippur (Hebrew) literally, "the Day of Atonement"; the gravest of Jewish holidays, in which the individual takes stock of his behavior in the world during the preceding year.

Zaddik (Hebrew, pl. *Zaddikim*) literally, "the righteous ones"; the spiritual masters, our guides.

INDEX